RECONNECTING TO WONDER AND AWE

A Spiritual Playbook for Bringing the Wisdom and Energy
of Your Soul into the Everyday to Create Your Best Life

Linda E. Grimm

BALBOA.PRESS

A DIVISION OF HAY HOUSE

Balboa Press books may be ordered through booksellers or by contacting:

Balboa Press
A Division of Hay House
1663 Liberty Drive
Bloomington, IN 47403
www.balboapress.com
1 (877) 407-4847

Because of the dynamic nature of the Internet, any web addresses or links contained in this book may have changed since publication and may no longer be valid. The views expressed in this work are solely those of the author and do not necessarily reflect the views of the publisher, and the publisher hereby disclaims any responsibility for them.

Interior Graphics/Art Credit: Revolution Studios for author's photo; All other artwork is the work of the author. It is Zentangle Inspired Art and not pure Zentangle®.

The author of this book does not dispense medical advice or prescribe the use of any technique as a form of treatment for physical, emotional, or medical problems without the advice of a physician, either directly or indirectly. The intent of the author is only to offer information of a general nature to help you in your quest for emotional and spiritual well-being. In the event you use any of the information in this book for yourself, which is your constitutional right, the author and the publisher assume no responsibility for your actions.

Print information available on the last page.

ISBN: 978-1-9822-3708-0 (sc)
ISBN: 978-1-9822-3709-7 (e)

Library of Congress Control Number: 2019916487

Balboa Press rev. date: 11/20/2019

♥

Your choice.
Your design.
Your creation.
Your art.
Your life.
What's your pleasure today?

♥

Table of Contents

What You Need to Know

Part One – The Foundation

Part Two – The Journey Begins

BE beautiful today! And have fun doing it!

What You Need to Know

♥

Your choice.
Your design.
Your creation.
Your art.
Your life.
What's your pleasure today?

♥

A Note from Me to You

I would love to share with you what is true for me right now. What I will share may seem far-fetched. But, what if it wasn't? What if, instead, it was designed to open you to possibilities that could change your life in fabulous ways, and do so easily?

Let me guide you to a spiritual perspective you may not have considered before. Let me guide you back to a connection with, and understanding of, your soul. When you allow that part of you to shine through you here and now, miracles happen. Life flows. Love flows. Wonderful abundance flows. Success flows. And, you sparkle!

Set what you think you know aside and let your heart guide you. I'm not here to convince you of anything. I am simply sharing my current truth with you. Take whatever makes your heart sing, your body move, and your mind smile.

You are your own guru. Own that. Let me show you how. Let's reconnect to wonder and awe, and Divine understanding dressed as childlike innocence. Step aboard this joyful ride with me and let's play!

♥ *When your soul shines through, miracles happen. Life flows. Love flows. Wonderful abundance flows. Success flows. And, you sparkle! I'm in. Are you?*

♥ *Divine understanding dressed as childlike innocence… What comes to mind when you read that? Hopefully, it brings to mind times when you were a child and you were filled with wonder and awe at what was presenting. That feeling is extending a hand out to your soul and saying "let's play together".*

♥

Your choice.
Your design.
Your creation.
Your art.
Your life.
What's your pleasure today?

♥

Introduction

Hello everyone! I am so excited to share with you what has been shared with me from Spirit. It is a 101 day experiential journey all about you. It is tailor-made for you because you are a part of the design! I offer you a focal point of consideration and experience for each of 101 days and you take it from there. Your experience and connection will be as rich and full and amazing and beautiful and joyful as you commit to and allow.

I want to reconnect you to your innate sense of wonder and awe. I want you to see life as a most amazingly exquisite and perfectly unfolding set of miracles, every moment of every day! I want you to see the tapestry of life. I want you to hear the symphony of life's siren song. I want you to breathe life in consciously and feel it energize and support and renew you. Because, as you shift back into that, you will remember that you are already enlightened. You really are.

Your soul is enlightened. My offering is to assist you in reconnecting to your soul energy and the energy of all life. From there, life looks different and your experience of life is different. It is loving and joyful and peaceful and compassionate and kind and fun and wonderfully abundant! So, please join

♥ *Would you like your life to be loving and joyful and peaceful and compassionate and kind and fun and wonderfully abundant? Would you like your intuitive gifts to beautifully flow to you without effort or conscious thought?*

me in exploring this gift of Spirit. Let me help you remember the feelings of wonder and awe in a fun and easy way that will open you to your full set of intuitive gifts and incredible joy.

We are all here for the journey. But, our understandings of what that journey is all about vary, sometimes quite dramatically. Our time together will be a joyful and moving journey of self-discovery, self-remembrance, self-empowerment, self-expansion, co-creation/creation, love, peace, truth, and the joy of Being you. (What more could one want?!) You are already enlightened! Let's reconnect to that truth and bring that understanding into the here and now.

This book is for those who are new to spiritual expansion and those who are well versed. For those of you who are new to this exploration and play, I hope it opens and expands you such that you desire more learning and play. And, for those of you who already have a solid spiritual foundation, we all know that there are times when we fall out of alignment, harmony, and balance. Sometimes, we desire a bit of assistance to help us realign. Going back to the basics, and/or discovering things you didn't get originally, can work wonders. I hope the offerings in this book will allow you to step out of where you are and back into joy and love and peace.

Many blessings of love and joy and peace,

Linda

♥ Our time together will be a joyful and moving journey of self-discovery, self-remembrance, self-empowerment, self-expansion, co-creation/ creation, love, peace, truth, and the joy of you.

How to Use This Book

The first part of the book will provide you with some background information about energy, creation, how it relates to art, beliefs, and feelings, and some other areas of thought that will give you a foundation for the second part of the book.

The second part of the book is the experiential part. I have divided it into three sections with every exploration/exercise building to the next, and each section doing the same.

♥ You are already enlightened.

You may be tempted to do what we've all done and not engage in the entirety of the experiences. They may be inconvenient upon occasion. Sometimes, you may just not feel like it. That's why I worked to make each focus pretty simple and easy. Of course, as they continue to build upon each other, you may find that you are encouraged to think of things throughout the day. You may think of that as cumbersome, but if you will keep the end goal in mind – reconnection to wonder and awe and your intuitive gifts – I believe you will see the benefit of doing your very best to stay with it. It's 101 days designed to reconnect you to joy and the wisdom and energy of your soul, in a safe and fun way. That should be a happy dance!

If you are an experienced spiritual explorer, you may find that you are tempted to skip over some of the first experiences because they seem so basic and so simple. I would urge you to not do so. They came to me as a progression. If you are reading this book, perhaps there are one or two that you missed somewhere along the way or that you would be well served to revisit. Please honor your time reading this book and give it a good old college try. I trust that you will receive what is best for your continued journey.

A friend of mine who was a runner said there were days when there would be ice on the streets, yet she would dress appropriately and go out to run. She was always glad she did. She said it was the act of deciding and then getting out the door that was the hardest part. She always enjoyed the run, even if in less than optimal conditions. She expected a good result and that's what she got. That was her advice to you. Just do it – you'll be glad you did.

♥ *You are the artist of your life.*

*Near the end of the 101 days as we explore and expand deep within, you may want more time for a particular day. Take it. This is about you learning about you and what makes you tick and what makes you happy. You may never have considered some of the expansions offered for you to explore. Be kind and gentle with yourself and love yourself enough to continue. Just know that each of these is offered to you as a gift from Spirit. If you're reading this now, these gifts are for you. I have complete faith that your time and attention will be handsomely rewarded!

The sections of the second part of the book are:

FIRST EXPANSION

First Expansion is designed to get you back in touch with childlike innocence, imagination, and carefree abandon. Reconnecting you with your body, the earth, your essence - and fun is the goal.

BEGINNING TO BELIEVE EXPANSION

The Beginning to Believe Expansion is designed to begin to take down the barriers to authenticity and living as who you really are.

TRUE SIGHT EXPANSION

True Sight Expansion is designed to unlock the doors to your heart. It is designed to allow you to safely be you. It is designed to help you to begin to fully allow the love of others to touch you deeply. For as you do that, so do you touch the authentic and most expanded version of you – the you that is part of the Divine Energy of Creation and thus, a part of all life.

♥ *You are a creator.*

There is an experience/exercise for each day for a little over three months. Each is a focus point for the day. *They are designed to reconnect you to love and joy and peace; to reconnect you to your body, the moment, and all that is around you; to reconnect you to your own Divinity – who and what you really are - and to open the channels to your beautiful intuitive gifts.* You are ALREADY enlightened. Truly. Yet, the focal point of you that is in the here and now does not always access the fullness and wholeness and amazingly wonderful richness of that. I want to help YOU change that for you. We will do that through fun and creative imagination and art.

♥ I hope you enjoy my "butterdragons" throughout this book. They are a cross between an art butterfly and an art dragonfly. They make me happy and that's all they are created to do. I share them with you so that you will see it doesn't have to take a lot to open to creativity and all that you are. All creativity is worthy and will accomplish what even the most magnificent will do.

This is not an art book just so you know. This is a book to open you to your inner guidance and consciously creating your life as you desire it. It's about you understanding that you are the artist of your life. It was conceived per the gifts and teachings (of a way to help others) that were shown to me by the Divine Energy of Creation. It is a beautiful, powerful, easy and fun way to help people and it came into being as Choice Point Creation Arts. Choice Point Creation is that point outside of time and space where you chose to come into this dimension and you chose experiences you wanted to have and how you wanted them to play out. However, from this more focalized perspective, what you chose and created doesn't always suit you. In comes the Arts portion. I have found that art soothes the soul. Art fosters creativity. And art helps to open the pathway to the Divine Energy of Creation – the energy of all life combined and of which you are both a part, and you ARE – in a safe and fun way. It lets down your self-imposed barriers. It allows you to feel what you may be missing in your conscious experiences.

You are the artist of your life. If you don't believe it now, I hope you will by the end of your engagement with this book and what it holds for you. I want you to believe and know that you are a creator and that you can dream and create and manifest what you desire. I want you to know your intuitive gifts and be able to use them in joyful, abundant, and compassionate ways. I want you to love life and love getting up every day ready to experience all the bounty, all the diversity, all the love, all the joy life has to offer – all in accordance with what you personally desire. You may not "get" it all now, but I trust what

I am sharing will open your ability to believe and open you to understanding a more expansive version of truth. Let me walk with you through the fun of releasing what no longer serves you and choosing what will. Ready?

Some people learn from the big picture. I'm giving you that. Some learn from experiences and doing. I'm giving you LOTS of that! And, almost everyone benefits from repetition of key points. I'm giving you that too – by design. Intentional design.

You will find that much of the information I am sharing with you overlaps and makes a lovely tapestry of understanding. Looking at it from multiple perspectives and in different ways helps you to retain and then use the information. I hope you will understand as I will repeat some things I've already shared (or change them up a little) for clarity, for retention, and to help you understand a new area of the foundation of you and your reality. We start now.

♥ *You and your soul are One. You have just forgotten for the moment. Let's change that!*

Throughout this book, there will be space available for you to write your thoughts, your feelings, and your inspirations if you desire to do so. This is a spiritual playbook. A playbook is an identified plan of action to get you to a desired goal, with strategies and insights and understandings to give you what you need to succeed and thrive. That's what you have here to help you connect to your Divine wisdom and the energy of that and all your intuitive gifts. And, lucky for us all, it's designed to be easy, fast, super fun, with lots of wonder and awe sprinkled around. Your wait for the second part of the book – the playbook strategies – will hopefully be like the anticipation of your favorite cheesecake or favorite ice cream ready for you to enjoy! Woohoo! I love that! So, take advantage of the space to jot down things that occur to you, if that resonates. You are receiving from the Divine as you read so you may become inspired and think of things you hadn't considered before. That's a win-win in my playbook!

Shared with love and gratitude,
Linda

Are you ready to have fun?

♥

Your choice.
Your design.
Your creation.
Your art.
Your life.
What's your pleasure today?

♥

Part One

The Foundation

♥

Your choice.
Your design.
Your creation.
Your art.
Your life.
What's your pleasure today?

♥

What Is the Divine Energy of Creation?

There is an energy that is in all of us and that connects all life. There are many names for this energy – God, Allah, Source, the Universe, Supreme Being, Elohim, Yahweh, Krishna, Ganesha, etc. I have chosen the name Divine Energy of Creation as a way to share with you my understandings of this energy and how to become consciously aware of and use this energy. I chose the name because of all the beliefs, feelings, ties, and expectations we have attached to familiar and regularly used names. We are all part of one energy – all life – plants, animals, everything. We are part of that energy and we ARE that energy. As such, we can access the entirety of that energy and all the truths and understandings therein. Are you open to believing that?

That may seem off the charts of probability to many of you. But, what if it wasn't? And what if I could give you a set of fun exercises/experiences that are easy to do that would bring you into alignment with your soul energy? Would you want to give it a try? It's about reconnecting to your sense of childlike wonder and awe. It's about being in the now. It's about believing in yourself and seeing yourself for who and what you

♥ *Everyone has the right to connect to the Divine Energy of Creation. The connection is direct unless you say, "not for me".*

really are – a Divine Being having a human experience. It's about connecting to creativity and art to show you that it is safe and fun and exhilarating to open that channel of connection and how incredibly powerful that is. It's about inviting your soul to walk hand-in-hand with you through 3D life (3 dimensional with width, height, and depth, which is how we view "reality" here and now), consciously creating as you go. Are you in?

♥ Did you know you are energy? As energy, you have an automatic relationship with other energy. Whether you know the science of that or not, it happens. The important thing to know is that if your energy is that of joy and love and peace, that is what will be attracted to you. The more you really feel that energy vs. just saying or desiring it, the more powerful an attractor it becomes.

How to Connect to the Divine Energy of Creation and Why You Would Want To

We have this feeling that in order to connect to our soul and the Divine Energy of Creation, we have to dress in robes, climb to the top of a mountain, shave our heads, and meditate 24/7. That's changed. Did you not get the memo?

Anyone can connect. We can all access our spiritual gifts. It may just take a bit of alignment with love and joy and peace to do so. An easy way is through art. You are creating your life as art right now. Most people are doing it subconsciously without knowing how it works, or that they have a choice. Is your "life art" of a color and texture and medium and vision that you would choose? If not, a bit of realignment with nature, your body, creativity, and seeing everyone as doing the best they can in any given moment with where they are physically, mentally, emotionally, and spiritually should do it for you.

When you are allowing the full connection to your soul and

♥ Would you rather react to life or consciously create your life?

♥ Anyone can connect to the Divine Energy of Creation. Pick up your "art and creativity" phone line and call home.

the Divine Energy of Creation, life flows. You are consciously aware that your thoughts and feelings are the building blocks of your future and you can consciously change them to raise your energetic vibration to create and manifest what you desire in the here and now. You begin to see your life as art that you are creating moment-to-moment. That's why it's important to reconnect to "living in the moment", instead of with your memories or your projections. When you are fully present and conscious of what you are thinking, feeling, saying, and doing, you have choice. You can then choose how you want your life to present and unfold for you. You no longer have to feel like you are reacting to life. Instead, you know you are creating your life and you can change those parameters that have been defined by your beliefs and feelings and patterns (developed over time by a wide variety of influences). You begin to pilot your own ship. And, it becomes easy and joyful and immersed in love and kindness and compassion and wonderful abundance in all areas of your life. Isn't it time you explored if this could work for you? I can show you how to reset.

♥ Who is piloting your ship? I hope you know!

♥ Did you know your thoughts and feelings are the building blocks of your future? What are you building right now? Is it the beautiful estate of which you've always dreamed?

What and Who Are You? (What is a Soul?)

You are a Divine Being. Yes, that's right – you! You are a part of the Divine Energy of Creation and you also ARE that energy. You retain your individualized expression of life and have choices you may make. Yet, you are simultaneously connected to all other life as the Whole of Creation. As such, you have all the wisdom and power and understanding of the whole – if you connect in through unconditional love. That most expanded version of you is your soul. You, here and now, are a focal point of expression. Your soul may have many focal points of expression happening simultaneously. That's what I believe "look within" really means. It means checking in with your soul. You "go back to" or "go within" your expanded soul self.

Did you know there is light within each cell of your body - within the mitochondria? Scientists call these biophotons. I believe that light is your *body's* energetic avenue to your soul. When your body dies, the focal point of you in the here and now goes back into the expansion of your soul. And, your body points of light (Light) – the individual cell connection to your soul within the mitochondria – dim and extinguish as your body dies. The Light of you goes home. (*More on this later.)

♥ *You are a Divine Being having a human experience.*

♥ *Here and now, you are a focal point of expression.*

You are a part of the Divine Energy of Creation – the energy of all life everywhere combined – and you ARE that energy. You are both a co-creator and a creator. You create your life and you can learn to do it consciously and deliberately. I'd LOVE to assist you.

♥ *Psst… You ARE the LIGHT.*

♥ *You can create your life consciously and deliberately.*

You Are Enough Right Now

You have many beliefs about who you think you are and what you believe you deserve. These beliefs come from a variety of sources. But, let's just cut to the chase.

♥ Actually, you're way more than enough! You're perfect just as you are!

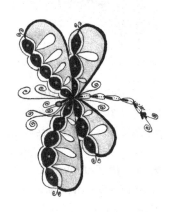

You ARE enough. Right now. That may sound strange to many. The concept of already being enough when you don't really feel you know who you are or what you are here to do can seem insurmountable. But, what if I again reminded you that you are Divine? What if I told you that you are part of and you ARE the Divine Energy of Creation – the energy of all life combined as One?

Your soul essence is whole and complete and requires nothing more. Your soul essence is that part of you that is fully aware and conscious of its connection to, and within, the energy of the whole – of all life – and feels that connection fully and completely.

There is a misconception that if you are part of a whole, you lose something. Most frequently, it is the sense that you lose at least part of your sense of self. You also lose control. You are at the whim of the whole and no longer have autonomy. But, what if those presumptions were incorrect? What if, instead, you acted as One without dissension, without avarice, without feeling the need to manipulate or control or oversee? What if, instead, whatever happened "birthed" from unconditional love and just was? And what if all expressions of the whole loved the result! Would you feel differently then?

You see, we tend to think of these things in three-dimensional terms – from the head. We base our presumptions on the programs* and beliefs running in our conscious and subconscious mind, many of which were formed in childhood! There is a much more expanded offering available to those who would open to it.

*Programs are beliefs that have been "verified" and categorized internally by your conscious and subconscious mind so often that they hold even more power than a single belief. When you develop a belief, your subconscious and your conscious mind are always looking for verification of the truth of that belief. When verification is found, whether true or not (because you are subjectively evaluating the veracity), it is added to that belief until it is "automatically" true and doesn't need to be authenticated again. Ultimately, this could mean that changing a program is more of an issue since there - quite likely - will be resistance to changing it. That's another reason why having a more direct pathway of communication with your soul is so wonderful. Your soul has the capability and know-how to change anything instantly - even pesky programs!

♥ Actually, you're way more than enough! You're perfect just as you are!

♥ Only that of love can be birthed from love. Nothing else is possible.

How to Live in the Sweet Spot or…How to Not Have an Unfortunate Day!

We're human so the adage goes. It is just in our nature to have things happen in a certain way. Well, you know what - yes and no to that. We are also Divine Creators. We have the capacity and capability to connect to our own inner Divinity. When we do that, we are consciously aware of the flow of the Divine Energy of Creation, the energy that flows through all things. When we are aware of that, we know we are part of the energy that creates.

♥ *Do you believe in you, or not?*

We have choice in this expression of life. We choose how we experience life. We, therefore, can choose to not follow the cultural, historical, and familial dictates of how life should work. We can change those dictates. By we, I mean you. You can change any part of it you choose so that you experience life as you desire.

Don't like what you have come to know as being human? Change it. We are told that certain things are absolutes. Are they really? Do you believe the Divine Energy of Creation can change anything? Yes? Well, if you are part of that energy, why can't you? "But I don't know how!" you say. What if I could help you? Would you want to try?

Your mind is an amazing gift. You consciously utilize only a tiny part of its amazing capacity. Your subconscious runs most things for you. How does it know what to choose for you? Well, you help it out by your interpretations of what happens to you and the resulting beliefs. For example, you touch a hot stove. It burns you. You then believe that touching a hot stove will burn you. Yet, you don't always come up with an understanding of what happens that is the most expanded truth. This is especially true when you are a child with a child's view and a child's experiences to draw from for the interpretation. Case in point... The parents of a young child know the child needs dental work. The parents take the child to the dentist. The child experiences the dental work as painful, uncomfortable, scary, and traumatic. The child may even register it as abuse, even if he or she doesn't know that word yet. The parents are supreme to a child. They provide food, water, shelter, comforts, safety, and love. Or do they? The child may now question that and may feel that the parents can't be trusted to look after the child's best interests. The parents took the child to a place where the child was traumatized, right? They approved it. They set it up. Can you imagine carrying around that belief for most of your life? That's right. Once that belief gets registered, it rarely gets re-examined until it comes into conflict with something you believe more. In the meantime, other beliefs build on that one. Can you see what a flimsy house of cards those beliefs would make?

♥ *When you change non-serving beliefs, you change your life.*

All that said, the subconscious catalogs beliefs and sorts them until it begins to run programs in the background based on them. From the above example, the child might come to the conclusion that "I always have to be on guard." How sad. Yet the beliefs keep supporting that as the child is made to go to school, eat vegetables, get vaccinated, go visit Auntie (No hate mail please! I'm an Auntie too!) ... you get the point I'm sure. The child may have long ago forgotten that initial visit to the dentist. But, the beliefs and feelings registered live on.

From time to time it's really good to do a housecleaning on the subconscious. You do that by examining your beliefs and asking yourself why you believe the way you do. Knowledge is power. If you know the cause, you can choose to no longer believe what before you knew as truth. When you change non-serving beliefs, you change your life.

If you want to live in that sweet spot, you need to learn how to recognize when you might have beliefs that no longer serve you. How do you do that? You observe what is happening in your life. Where are those places where you are not happy, not peaceful, not engaged in life in the best possible way? That's a clue that you should look RIGHT THERE. It will show up in your life first and, eventually, if you choose to ignore it long enough, it will manifest in the physical. Your choice.

♥ *Beliefs build upon each other. If the initial belief doesn't serve you, how likely is it that the belief building blocks that come from it are serving you? No worries, though! We can change beliefs!*

Let me give you an example. Say you're having money issues. You are having difficulty getting enough money together to pay your bills. Begin to look at your beliefs about money. You can start with common sayings about money like "Money is the root of all evil." Well, yikes! If money is the root of all evil, why would you want to attract and have more money? Then begin to look at what would happen if you had lots of money. Would all your family be lined up at the door with their hands held out? If so, perhaps you are energetically limiting your ability to have enough money because you don't want to have to deal with that. Why are you scared of dealing with that? Well, maybe it is because if you told them "no" you think they wouldn't love you anymore and would leave you. Whatever those beliefs are, you need to be the excavator on the archeological dig of your beliefs and get them on the table to be dealt with. Once you know what they are, you then can choose which way you want to go as you move forward.

♥ *"Living in the sweet spot... sounds awesome!"*

When you feel empowered, when you feel like you actually have the ability to choose for your life, you begin to know what it feels like to live in the sweet spot. As you embrace that and do it more and more - guess what! - vibrationally you begin to attract more of that into your life.

We are energy. We are a bunch of molecules held together by our beliefs. A vibration of that energy will attract more of the same to it - kind of like a tuning fork. So, choose what you want to attract and know in your heart of hearts that it is on its way. It will come.

If you need outside verification of your beliefs (temporarily!), you can use "energy testing" (sometimes known as applied kinesiology or muscle testing) to check those beliefs. Often, we are really surprised at what our subconscious believes! We would have bet money that we didn't believe that! We would have lost.

What Is Healing?

What a wonderful question! And what a complex answer I could give. Yet, let's see if I can make this as simple as possible. I believe "healing" is becoming realigned, harmonized, and balanced with your soul and the Divine Energy of Creation. I believe dis-ease and dis-order and maladies of any type are merely expressions from the soul letting you know that you are not aligned and that you may want to look into where there are beliefs, thoughts, feelings, and patterns that are keeping you from that alignment. "Oy vey!" you may exclaim right about now! I get it.

♥ *Become best friends forever with your soul.*

But, what if I told you that I had a relatively simple way to realign you that you would enjoy? Too good to be true, you might be thinking. However, I have seen success and wonderful results with happiness and joy. No! It can't be that simple, right? Well, actually, it can. Joy is one of the highest vibrations and one of the vibrations most closely aligned to your soul energy. The more you can enjoy joy, the more your cells shift into that vibration and the less able lower vibrations are capable of keeping a foothold.

Lists of emotions, in order of the distress they cause within the body, abound. An easy online search will give you lots of

choices. But, you can make your own. Begin with fear as the emotion that is most detrimental. End with love. All the other emotions fall in between on a graduated scale. They would be things like guilt, unworthiness, shame, apathy, anger, hate, courage, kindness, joy, peace, etc. They all fall within fear and love. Not all lists will begin and end as my list does. That's ok. We all are where we are, and we all have our own thoughts and understandings and things to share. It's all good. Some things you will automatically resonate with, and some you won't. I think that's pretty amazing, actually!

I believe fear is the core component of any distress and/or misalignment. It may be fear that is hidden or very interwoven with other things, but it is still fear. Often, it is interlinked with safety and your ability to feel safe in the world and within your surroundings. I believe fear is the base of disease.

My recommendation is to always look for the good in everything. Be as happy as you can manage every moment of every day. I intend to teach you how to do that through the daily experiences set out for you within this book.

Your beliefs and the associated feelings, both conscious and subconscious, impact the flow of energy throughout your body. For every stimulus you encounter, there are chemical and electrical impulses sent by the brain throughout your body to tell the body how to act (fight or flight or freeze). When there is conflict between your subconscious and conscious beliefs, a series of chemical and electrical impulses go into overdrive and clog up the neural pathways and the synapses where the signals have to "jump" to continue their journey as messengers to the cells of the body. A temporary overabundance of these signals is not harmful. However, when there is conflict between your beliefs, the brain doesn't know what to do and it keeps going "Danger, Danger, Danger!" At some point, the natural flow of energy is impeded by the overflow of signals and begins to back up. It is at this juncture that disease begins to show.

Finding the cause of the conflict and clearing it is a lovely remedy. Begin with where the dis-ease is located. What is it trying to tell you? If you are experiencing allergies, what is irritating you? If you feel achy and heavy, where are you seeing life as a burden? It can be an interesting puzzle. There are books available that will list various maladies and a likely set of beliefs for them. An easy online search will offer you many choices. My goal is to help you become aware that your body is your partner. Your body is your friend. Without it, your experiences right now would be quite different. You chose this. I want to help you enjoy it!

(A note here: We tend to judge everything. I want you to know that perhaps not every malady is a direct result of something from this particular time of the expression of you – in other words, there are other potential implications from other "lifetimes" of you and other influences outside of your current beliefs that may be at play. That's something for you to delve into another time. I just want to alert you that, *typically*, if you have dis-ease of any type, find the core issue bothering you and release it and your malady will disappear. But, sometimes that is not the case. Don't be overwhelmed. This is just a heads-up so that if it doesn't go away through your spiritual efforts, you

♥ Dis-ease and dis-order and maladies of any type are merely expressions from the soul letting you know that you are not aligned. Are you paying attention?

will know that it may be more interwoven and intricate than "just a belief reset". Don't think that with the information I am sharing here that you can "diagnose" the beliefs for someone else automatically. There may be more, and until you are able to fully connect to the Divine Energy of Creation in pure love and ask, change may not happen. And, I encourage you not to judge yourself or others as you find distress. It's not about that. It's about self-discovery and holding a steady vibration in resonance with joy and love and peace.

As your natural flow of life-force energy and the natural flow of inner and outer information is able to get to you unimpeded and unobstructed, your body does not go into the fight or flight response. This results in clear focused information from both internal and external stimuli and from intuitive sources.

♥ *Fear is the most detrimental emotion. Love is the most cohesive and healing. What do you fear the most? Why do you fear it? When do you remember first knowing you had the fear? What was happening in your life then? Knowledge is the first step in real change.*

So, the bottom line is to have conflicting beliefs auto-resolve. That comes from living in joy because the vibration and energy of joy will not sustain the energy of conflict and distress. Entrainment also applies here. Entrainment is about two or more rhythmic cycles synchronizing. Things will begin to vibrate in sync with the most expanded (highest) resonance available, given time. That means if you begin to live in joy, you will be providing that as the "tuning fork" for you. If you sustain that vibration, everything in your life will attune to it or leave.

Take a moment to be happy. No matter what your situation is or how you are feeling about things, pause. Take a deep breath and remember what it feels like to be happy. Let that feeling fill you completely. Then, choose to be grateful that you know what happiness feels like and choose to allow it to be in your day today. Happiness matters. YOU matter. What you feel matters. Choose to have happy moments and really feel it in each moment. Then, remember that you have choices. You can choose to allow yourself to be within the vibration of happiness even as you take care of everyday matters. The more you resonate with, and are in the vibration of joy and happiness, the more you attract the same.

Happy happy joy joy gratitude gratitude and then more happy... and joy...

* See *Emotions* under "Some of My Favorites" at the end of the book for more information about the body holding and being an indicator of emotions.

♥ *Happy happy joy joy gratitude gratitude and then more happy... and joy...*

Happiness vs. Joy

♥ *If you put limits on your happiness, joy won't have an invitation to the party.*

♥ *Happiness is worn. Joy is lived.*

To me, there is a difference between happiness and joy. Happiness is "caused" by something. Joy is pervasive and is an infusion of a feeling that is so a part of you that you radiate the vibration of it just by BEing it, experiencing it, and allowing it. *Happiness is worn. Joy is lived.*

So, how does one elevate happiness to joy? That's a good question! Happiness doesn't always lead to joy, but it may. If you think of happiness as a preview of what a taste of joy might be like and you allow happiness to shift your cells into anticipation of the next taste, your cells can be trained to "seek out" that feeling. As you experience more and more happiness, you begin to allow joy – in its fullness and richness of Spirit – to fill you and nurture you and embrace you and flow from you to others. That, in turn, begets happiness, just as happiness has the potential to beget joy. Happiness can birth joy within you if you will allow it to expand and bring you peace and security. Joy can birth happiness when you allow it to be focused on activities that you love.

A wonderful way to work with this concept and see it in action is art. Art can be of any type that causes you to become fully immersed in it, where time disappears and all you know is your creative nature in action. That level of connection helps to open the pathway to your soul self. That connection is the road back to unlimited joy. The more you travel that road, the more joy travels with you. Then, at some point, you stay in that state and vibration of joy all the time. You attract more joy and you help others to find their road to joy. Art is a fantastic travel companion! It can put you on the superhighway to joy.

Explore your favorite art as an opening to connection. Allow your creative nature to flow without filters and without barriers. Get used to what it feels like to effortlessly and joyfully create. When you do, you will find you can automatically get back to that feeling – and the connection – even without the art. It's a beautiful way to reintroduce yourself to your soul, with a conscious understanding of the connection. From there, you can begin to create your life – using that same energy – moment-to-moment.

Happy creating! Happy joyful day!

♥ *Happiness is a preview of what a taste of joy might be like.*

♥ *Full immersion in art opens a pathway to your soul. It is the road back to unlimited joy. Art is a fantastic travel companion!*

Authenticity and Living an Authentic Life

♥ Are you living your life as you?

In order to be in full alignment with your soul in the here and now, and be able to feel and know and experience with the eyes of the soul fully and completely, you have to be living an authentic life. By that I mean you should be living your truth - what you really believe and know at the moment - in all areas of your life.

What tends to happen is that people do this in stages. Perhaps they are authentic in their spiritual life. Perhaps they are authentic in their life as a parent. But perhaps they are not as authentic as a life partner, or perhaps not in the work environment. At some point on that spiritual journey, the Divine will say "Hey, there is going to be an unscheduled rest stop right here until you clean house and become aligned in all the areas of your life." For many, this will be a big shock. It will seem like multiple, not so wonderful feelings and/or issues pop up all at once. It tends to leave one feeling confused and disheartened and overwhelmed and ready to give up.

Here's what is happening. You, as you progress spiritually and become authentic in any way, begin to raise your vibration. The more you align with your true self, your soul, and begin living that level of understanding and truth in your daily life, the more your inner Divinity begins to surface and shine. There comes a point where the vibration you have reconnected to becomes so great that anything unauthentic is no longer supported. In other words, you cannot continue to progress and become brighter, more attuned, more intuitive, more aligned with the Divine Energy of Creation's highest truth and still have areas of your life based within the paradigm defaults of fear, anger, hate, mistrust, and the like. Your vibration will not sustain that division within you.

This may show up as your life appearing to fall apart. Those things and people who do not support your alignment with your own Divinity will be brought forward into the limelight of your life to show you the discrepancy - the non-alignment. This typically presents as chaos, distress, trauma, drama, and/or dis-ease of various types. This is not necessarily a bad thing! These are indicators. These are red flags. These are your guideposts to positive change and forward movement.

You want to continue to explore and grow spiritually, right? Use these indicators to your advantage! Ask yourself "What are they here to show me?" "How can I use what is going on to guide me into a more peaceful and loving and aligned life?" When you can step outside of the trauma and drama long enough to view the events without the emotions of them, you will usually be able to see where in your life you are misaligned. When you are willing to do this, the Divine will help you by bringing the right people into your circle, bringing you the right books and shows, helping you to see and know what to do and how to do it. You may find it helpful to consult

♥ *The energy of your soul does not support inauthenticity.*

with an energy healer or spiritual counselor who is trained in ways to assist you with changing those underlying default patterns. Meditation is good, with an intention of receiving clarity with full conscious awareness of what is needed to shift your situation to one of grace and harmony and balance. As I mentioned, when you are ready and willing to make these changes, the Divine will support you and the right people and understandings will flow into your life without effort.

♥ The Divine Energy of Creation knows the truth about you and still loves you unconditionally. Isn't that all you need?

So, if things aren't joyful and peaceful and abundant and if you aren't happy to be alive every day, look at where you are not being authentic. Where is it that you betray yourself by not speaking your truth, by hiding who you are and what you believe, by not letting others know what you need to feel and be honored and respected as a person of worth? Where are you living the lie? Where are you not being authentic – i.e. who and what you really are? No lying to yourself. The Divine Energy of Creation sees you. The Divine knows. The only one hearing the lies will be you. That won't serve you in the most expanded and best way. If your life is crumbling down around you and you look at it and say, "I don't see how any of this relates to me," that might be a good sign that deep down you don't want to look at yourself and how you feel about yourself. It might be a good time to ask for help. There is no shame in asking for help. Everyone needs it from time to time. If you aren't making progress with changing what isn't working in your life, pause. Take a moment and really look at what your life events are pointing out to you. If you can't see it, get a fresh outside perspective because, chances are, even if these particular events resolve, more will be on their way until you are willing to look.

Now, you can choose to stay in the trauma and drama and illness. It's your choice. You may think that looking deeply into your soul will be more painful. Know though that you will stay in this space - in this chaotic stagnant energy - until you do look. The vibration is unsupported by the higher joyful love-filled vibrations. If you are on an active spiritual journey and this has happened, you may feel like you are standing still for a time. However, as more and more people make the shift into the higher vibrations of energy, you will begin to feel like you are falling behind as you compare your life to what is happening in the lives of others. This will continue until the *Hundredth Monkey Effect** happens and everyone "remaining" finally has the understanding needed to make the change and shift into a higher vibrational frequency. Everyone will get there. It's whether or not you choose to stay immersed in the defaults of fear and anger until those remaining all shift together. Your choice.

♥ *Authenticity is the natural state of things.*

Authenticity. Authenticity - the full alignment with your Divinity and all that brings - brought into your daily life and practices will bring you much joy and good abundance and peace. It's the natural state of things. It's a reflection of who and what you truly are. You are a Divine BEing. You are one expression of the Divine. You can have all that represents - all that is - now. How? By coming into alignment with your authentic self and then BEing that authentic self in all ways, now. It's not as difficult as you may think. Think of what you love, what makes you happy. That's who you are. Bring that into everything you think, say, and do. Stay aligned with that. When you practice this, whenever you fall out of alignment, you will notice it immediately. Whatever it is won't make you feel happy and joyful and awesome. It's then your conscious choice whether to change that or to stand still as life swirls around you. Your soul is calling. You're on speed-dial. Are you going to pick up or not? I hope you do!

*Hundredth Monkey Effect
"The hundredth monkey effect is a purported phenomenon in which a new behavior or idea is claimed to spread rapidly by unexplained means from one group to all related groups once a critical number of members of one group exhibit the new behavior or acknowledge the new idea." (Wikipedia 2019)

♥ *You and your soul are One. You have just forgotten for the moment. Let's change that!*

The Foundations of Life as I See Them

There are several foundational levels that construct our perceived reality.

The first ones are the four pillars of:

Love
Peace
Joy
Truth

♥ *A house of cards is easily blown down. Make your foundation solid.*

These pillars are part of your very essence and act as a guide for you to use to navigate your earthly experience. They are there for you to gauge your experiences and feelings related to them, and to evaluate how aligned you are with your soul and the Divine Energy of Creation.

<u>Love</u> is unconditional and without limits, expectations, boundaries or confines of any kind. It just is.

<u>Peace</u> is that complete trust that you are safe, you are loved, you are valued and valuable, and you are a part of the Divine

Energy of Creation, and that you have full access to the whole of that simultaneously.

Joy is the feeling of pure bliss that flows to and through you as you acknowledge the truth of love and peace.

And, Truth is the most expanded version of the understanding and wisdom and knowing of the Divine Energy of Creation – not a point on the continuum of truth but the entirety of it, with pure understanding and the ability to use that truth to create.

Another set of foundational pillars are:

♥ *Love. Peace. Joy. Truth. These pillars are rock solid.*

Beliefs
Understandings
Definitions
Feelings

These pillars help define what you experience as reality in your earthly experience.

A Belief is what you believe about any given thing. Beliefs are formed in a variety of ways, some consciously, some not. They form an internal operating system for how you automatically react to situations and others.

Understandings are your interpretations of those beliefs. If two people say "I love myself," the interpretation of each about what that means could be vastly different based on each person's understanding of love and the understanding of self. Understandings often develop through experience. And, experience is often channeled by beliefs.

Definitions are statements that attempt to provide a framework of reference and meaning and/or identify essential qualities. They allow us to communicate more fluidly and have shared understandings. If you compare apples to oranges, what type of result would you expect to get? Not a very valid one! When you align your definition of things with the definition of the Divine Energy of Creation, you are able to look at things from the perspective of an even baseline. You can compare apples to apples and oranges to oranges. Your evaluation, then, is more valid.

Feelings are a combination of our emotional state and the corresponding physical sensations in any given moment. Feelings are often forgotten as individuals strive to figure out what is not working well. Feelings are the fuel for beliefs. Feelings are the current that allows your internal operating system to run. When you shift a belief or understanding or definition by choice, you are hoping to feel better. Yet sometimes, all your beliefs and understandings and definitions are all aligned and in balance, but you still don't feel better. It is because feelings can become infused within beliefs and they are entangled within other related beliefs (i.e. they build upon one another and can get "tangled" up together where it is hard to resolve and release just one). So, it is important to check in with the feelings you have related to experiences and to people. Look deeper than the surface. How do you really feel vs. how you think you should feel or how you want others to believe you feel? For something to have a positive shift for you, the feelings must shift in a positive way as well. If you are being honest with yourself, when you shift a belief in a positive way, the feeling will most likely shift in a positive way as well.

♥ *Feelings are the current that allows your internal operating system to run.*

These foundations provide you with a framework from which to experience life on earth. They offer support and a reliable indication of what is going on and how to remedy any areas that are not to your liking. Use them as the tools they are meant to be.

Ask yourself, does this situation (person, thing, etc.) make me feel loved or offer love? Does it bring me joy? Am I peaceful with it and how it is playing out? Does it feel like there is anything other than truth involved?

♥ Where is your foundation shaky? What can you do right now to change that?

When beliefs aren't working for you, they typically show up as physical ailments or uncomfortable or distressing situations. If you ask how the issue is serving you, you can then use the situation as a tool to help you uncover beliefs, understandings, definitions, and feelings that no longer serve you. They can then be changed. (Hang in there on the "how". Even more is coming in the second half of the book!)

If the situation is a physical ailment, use the location and type of ailment to alert you as to the root cause. For example, if you suddenly develop a sore throat, ask yourself "Where am I afraid to speak my truth?" If you develop a catch in your knee, ask yourself "Am I afraid to move forward in my life or my relationship or my whatever?" You can view these things as gifts from the Divine Energy of Creation to help you find clarity and truth. Once you identify the core cause of the distress within your beliefs and your feelings about those beliefs, and you deal with the initial formation of those beliefs and feelings, you may find that the ailment/situation "magically" disappears. When you shift the core of the issue, the energetic results then no longer have a negative impact on the chemical and electrical systems within the body and frequently the issue will instantaneously disappear.

As with any structure, the foundation is key. When you keep your foundation strong and solid, your life experience will follow suit.

♥ *And so it is if you allow it to be…*

Feelings – A Bit More on this Fuel of Creation

♥ *Do you believe you are responsible for what you feel? Are you a victim or a creator? Your choice.*

Feelings. Do you cringe when you read this word? Many do. And why would that be? Because to feel makes whatever is being experienced be truly real and a part of your reality. On some level, you know you are responsible for what you feel. If the feeling is not one of joy or love or like vibration, the part of you that knows your part in the vibration wants to shut down, hide the feeling as if it did not exist. The lower vibration of it hurts. The lower vibration of it, on some level, instills guilt and remorse and pain. Yet, we don't think we have the resources to change that. What a dilemma.

Or not.

Many people identify feelings as things. Feelings are not things. And, funny enough, feelings can identify as burdens, as weights, as very real things. Therefore, we have a set-up for a push-pull relationship with feelings. This sets up because we have an understanding of feelings that is not the most whole and comprehensive.

What if feeling was a way of BEing? What if feeling was a way of allowing the expressions of the heart as a conduit to the most expanded and comprehensive expression of ourselves – our soul? What if feeling and feelings were viewed as a connection to the soul and to our beliefs about ourselves, known or as yet unknown? What if we could use feeling and feelings as a tool for wholeness and wellness of body, mind, and Spirit? What if feeling and feelings are what life is truly about?

If all this were true, would you want to suppress them? Would you want to manipulate them? Would you want to control them? Or, would you truly accept each and every one, and allow them to guide you, to teach you, to free you from limitations and lack?

♥ *What if feeling was a way of Being?*

You are a powerful amazing beautiful part of the wholeness of the One, a co-creator/creator of your destiny, your story, your experiences, your life. Embrace the responsibility of that as a personalized gift of Spirit to you. For so it is and so you will experience it as such if you allow it to be and embrace it as your truth…

♥ *You are the co-creator/creator of your destiny, your story, your experiences, your life.*

The Continuum of Truth or Where Does Truth Come From

♥ *It's all about perspective.*

Let's start at the bottom line. The bottom line is that everything is the Divine Energy of Creation/Source/God/Creator/Allah/the Universe/etc. All life is part of the same universal unified whole. All of it. We are all part of the entirety of all creation AND we are that energy. That means that related to the perspective of truth, everything is truth. Yet, there can be variations and distortions and misrepresentations of truth depending on perspective.

So, how do you know what to believe? If you go to the Divine Energy of Creation, then you have all the collective knowledge, all the collective experiences, all the learning, all the wisdom from the energy that creates worlds and life as we know it. Within that energy resides all life and all that life brings.

You might envision this concept as a set of concentric circles. Within each circle is a range of understanding, and hence, truth. Encompassing all the circles, and all within each, is the largest circle. The totality of that is the Divine Energy of Creation energy.

Within each circle of understanding, all is truth. Yet, it is not the most expanded and comprehensive and all-inclusive understanding of truth. But, it is truth. It brings to mind a simple parable. If you put a man without sight at the trunk of an elephant and one at the back of an elephant, their understandings of the elephant would be vastly different. Yet, each would be real and true.

What if you envisioned those concentric circles as a spiral instead? At the widest expanse would be the ever-expanding Divine Energy of Creation. At the smallest expanse would be the least inclusive understanding. If you took that spiral and straightened it out, you would have the equivalent of a line. That could be considered your "continuum of truth". You can plug in on that continuum at any place and your understanding of truth would be different - sometimes to a great extent, and sometimes not. Your truth is dependent on your understandings and experiences and beliefs and feelings and your allowances i.e. what you are ready, willing, able, and think you deserve to allow into your conscious awareness. All that impacts your frequency and vibration. Your vibration will rise the more closely you are aligned with love and the entirety of the Divine Energy of Creation and that, in turn, allows you to access and accept a more expanded version of truth. This continuum is applicable to all life.

♥ *We are all part of the entirety of all creation AND we are that energy.*

At some point along that continuum, the messages begin to go more and more to ONLY ones of love and joy and peace. And peace in this context is not peace vs. non-peace. It is about allowing yourself to fully relax into love and joy without any fear or concern or hesitation. I hesitate to use words like "surrender" or "being vulnerable" because we tend to have a lot of beliefs attached to those words and most are not positive. But the peace of which I am speaking is like when you let out a huge sigh and just fully and completely relax without a worry or care in the world.

There are a lot of people standing on spiritual platforms these days. Some say they are talking to angels. Some say they have guides from other planets. Some say they are connecting to the soul. They all have a message and those messages may be conflicting. The reason is that the truth they are sharing is dependent on their individual vibration, the vibration of the conduit for the information, and where on the continuum the information related to a truth is "housed" and/or experienced. Even if someone is connecting to an enlightened spirit, that spirit may or may not be allowing and/or capable of accepting - yet - the MOST expanded truth of Divine energy. To compound things, the person on the platform may not - yet - be able to receive all of the truth from where they are connected and/ or they may misinterpret it. And, sometimes the information being shared is so outside the 3D norm it is hard to fit it into enough boxes to have it make sense, so it gets "embellished" or "decorated". In other words, the person interpreting the information may add or subtract parts to help with the understanding for others, but without clearly identifying what parts are embellished.

We tend to judge messages based on a variety of things, such as how many of our friends are buying in, what famous people are interested, what the person delivering the message is like, etc. However, that is 3D thinking. When you listen

♥ *Would you rather have your truth be a point on the continuum of truth or an understanding that encompasses the entire continuum of truth?*

to a message/truth, they are all from the Divine Energy of Creation – even the fake ones. Given that, trust that your soul-self will alert you to messages that resonate with where you are, or where it is time for you to be on that continuum of truth. Listen with your heart. How do you feel when you hear the message?

There is a caveat to going with just feelings, though. If you are ready or on the verge of being ready to expand your understanding of truth, you may get a twinge in your gut when you listen to some messages. That could mean two things. It could mean "run away" because the message is not for you, or it could mean that you fear taking the next step in your spiritual progression. So, what should you do if you are open to a message but get that twinge? Ask. * And then be sure to wait for the answer! So often the question is asked, but the person wants that answer immediately. Give it a chance to come in and yourself a chance to uncover it. In the meantime, take the message and put it on hold until you get clarity. It will wait if it is indeed a more expanded truth for you or one that is best for you to continue to pursue.

The thing to remember is… it's all truth. It's just truth from different viewpoints on that continuum, with interpretation added in. It may be the most expanded truth on a topic, and it may not. There are some topics where the 3D mind does not have the capacity to engage the most expanded truth. What is truth for you today may not be truth for you tomorrow, and that's normal and perfectly fine! That's why people with spiritual platforms can have such divergent messages and areas of focus. Some may talk of sacred geometry. Some

♥ *It's all truth. But the truth around us comes from different viewpoints on the continuum of truth, with interpretation added in. A truth may be the most expanded truth on a topic, or it may not. The more you are able to expand into your soul energy, the more you may know the most expanded version of truth.*

may talk of aliens. Some may talk of the planets and stars. Some may not bring up any of that. And, on some level, all are truth. It just depends. And, just to be clear, all of those points of reference are valid and valuable and are available to use to heighten your overall understanding of life and to assist you in being able to and willing to access even more expanded understandings. Because, as each life continues to experience and learn, the understanding and truth of the whole, the Divine Energy of Creation/Source/Creator/God/Allah/etc. also expands. So, all viewpoints are relevant.

It's important not to judge. Just know that the person with the message has his or her own place on the continuum of truth and each person attracts like energy in Spirit. Their point on the continuum may not be aligned with where your truth is in the moment. That's just fine. Find a person with a message that resonates with you, with your heart. Allow the others to just BE, without your commentary or judgment. The messages are fine for someone or they wouldn't be on their platform – even those that are made up. Those are truth too – just at a less expanded view of the entirety of truth. Those who are less than honest with what they offer have something to teach those who are drawn to them – it just may not be what either party believes it to be. Perhaps what they offer is allowing a listener to come to know proper discernment and how to identify with resonance. There is a reason that those who are not honest even have a platform and that people are drawn to them. That is the truth part - the understanding that all things are Divine and even what we would deem dishonest is serving a purpose for both sides, hopefully temporarily.

♥ If you have the most expanded version of truth, you know judgment serves no purpose. Allow others to have their experiences even if they are not served by your current truth. Choose compassion. Choose love. Release judgment. Without all the information since before the beginning of time, judgment is flawed. And, if you had all the information since before the beginning of time, judgment is irrelevant and not possible. Just saying…

Now that you have an understanding of all this, envision the straight-line continuum back as the spiral or concentric circles, knowing that truth is ever expanding and continuing since life continues forever.

Be willing to allow the most expanded truth. Open your understanding, open your heart, open your doors to the most expanded truth and reality for your best life now, and envision it all infused with beautiful love and the sparkling energy of joy and the blissfully relaxing energy of peace. For so it is if you allow it to be...

Asking will be discussed more in-depth in the Chapter *Changing Beliefs and "Asking"*.

♥ *Truth is ever changing for you moment-to-moment. View it as a learning avenue and not a fault. On some level, you already have ALL the truth there is in the moment.*

Living in the Moment

Life is here now. It's not spending time on a mountain top for years meditating. It's not in the space where you go when you meditate. It's not somewhere else. It's right where you are right now!

As we develop spiritually, we tend to look at the woes of the world and the woes of our life and our past and choose to focus on the "woo-woo". We tend to dream of what we touch upon in meditation. We tend to choose that over the here and now. And, who can blame anyone for that? It's much more beautiful. It's much more peaceful. It's much more joyful. It's much more loving. Or is it?

At the choice point of creation, we chose to come to earth; we chose how we would experience this life; we chose how we would be "cloaked" as we did so. We chose. And, we've spent lifetimes exploring those self-imposed, self-injected, barriers and limitations and un-truths – for the fun and experience of it.

But, now, as the brilliant creatures we are, we are becoming weary of that. We want more. We want something different. We want to be inspired. We want to be engaged in life once again. But, it all seems so dismal and so bleak and so hopeless. But, is it?

♥ *Does creating your life seem like too much responsibility? If not you, who is responsible? What would cause you to desire what you already own – your conscious creative ability to have your best life ever?*

Many now are learning how to get back in touch with the highest truth. We are learning that we truly are Divine expressions of the Energy of All Creation. *We are learning that all we have ever done and all we have ever experienced is not the truth of us, but just our exploration of this life and its expression as we have chosen it to be at the choice point of creation.*

In reconnecting, we are beginning to see a new way to play. What if we brought our gifts of the Divine into the here and now in full complement, in full force, with full expression? Now that's a thought! Well, woohoo! I say! Wouldn't that be an awesome way to continue to explore and play? What if we could consciously create moment-to-moment?

♥ *We are learning that all we have ever done and all we have ever experienced is not the truth of us, but just our exploration of this life and its expression as we have chosen it to be at the choice point of creation.*

Now at first, our ego gets super excited and envisions lovely ways of pay-back. Right? Lovely ways to pay ourselves back for all the trauma and drama we have ever experienced... but, that's the catch. If we allow our thoughts and our ego to drive our imagined choices, guess what happens? It doesn't resonate with the Divine Energy of Creation and we cannot connect sufficiently to make use of all the energy there is – all at once – which is what is required to consciously and instantly create our reality moment-to-moment. That, and being willing to allow it into creation, here and now.

And, with that understanding begins our journey to release and forgive and clear and transform our pathway to an understanding of ourselves as Divine Beings and the highest truth on why we came here to begin with. We begin to understand that, at our core, there is nothing but love. It is not possible to hate. It is not possible to want revenge. It is not possible to feel unworthy. For none of that is compatible with the energy of the highest truth of you. It just isn't.

We also begin to understand that, at the core of everyone else and at the core of all life, there is only love. It's not a platitude. It's the most expanded truth. As we begin to comprehend this and begin to allow it to become a part of our conscious truth, we can begin to love others regardless of what they say or do. *You begin by loving that core.* You begin by seeing that part of them - their core - as Divine love and acknowledging only that part of them. You then shift into being able to acknowledge that their actions and words that are anything other than non-egoic unconditional love, are fear-based. As you shift to that, you begin to open a pathway of compassion. It doesn't condone actions and words that are hurtful or harmful or mean. It merely sees a higher truth. It sees the base of fear and it sees the actions and words as shields. You begin to become more consciously connected to the Divine Energy of Creation. Your heart begins to let down its guard, its shields, its barriers. Because, in the most expanded truth, you know there is so much more. You know there is only love. This is where you are experiencing the continuum of truth as one whole. This is where you don't plug into a point on the continuum, you become all of it and know all of it.

Yes, I know that as you are immersed fully in the here and now that can seem so lame, so tired, so kumbayaish. I mean really – how long have we been singing that song? And, how's that been working for us? Seriously?

♥ *What if we could consciously create moment-to-moment?*

But, over time, those edges have softened for many and the desire for a more peaceful and loving, yet exciting and adventurous, life has become a siren song. Each generation shifts a bit.

In the big picture, time is irrelevant. It is not impactful because it is a construct of our experience on earth. Though, for us here right now, it seems like FOREVER and the despair and hopelessness flow in. Yet, some have persevered. And through their experiences and through their teachings and through their sharing, more and more of us have come to experiment with furthering our connection to Divine energy – but not as a servant and not as someone un-empowered, but as a PART of the Divine and a worthy part at that. Woohoo!

♥ *At the core you, at the core of everyone else, and at the core of all life, there is only love.*

The thing is, even that can become a siren song. People get so wrapped up in the "woo-woo" that they forget (or choose not to remember) that they are here now and it is important to be in the now and experience the now. But Voilà! Our amazing minds allowed us the tiny seed of a thought about a new way to experience. What if we could consciously create our everyday life? What if we could choose our daily experiences now – consciously? What if we could bring the wholeness of who and what we are in our highest expression into the now? Wouldn't that be a blast? Wouldn't that be so much fun? Wouldn't that provide a completely new platform from which to exist and BE and learn and experience?

Well, it's happening. In real-time. And, you can learn how to do the same. Are you all in?

Learn to focus in the now because you will learn that from that space, your beliefs and thoughts and feelings are building your future. You will learn that you can consciously guide that process. Would you like to go there? Let's party!

♥ *When you know as fact, and in your heart of hearts, that there is only love, you are experiencing the continuum of truth as one whole.*

We Are Energy

We are energy. Energy reacts to energy in fairly predictable ways. You are a many-layered Being. You are "operating" within the energy output of your heart, your brain, the earth, the Universe, and all other life. The interplay between these energies is not something most people are focused upon. Yet, they are there working in the background as you go about your day.

♥ *You are "operating" within the energy output of your heart, your brain, the earth, the Universe, and all other life.*

Your own energy is "adjusted" by many factors. Beliefs – both conscious and subconscious – are a major factor. Feelings play a part. Experience, patterns, defaults, and learning all factor in. I would also add in your expectations, which are developed per all of the above. Energy can fluctuate moment-to-moment.

Your brain communicates with your heart and your heart communicates with your brain. These communications impact your cognitive functioning and your emotional state in real-time. When you are experiencing the positive emotions of love and joy and like emotions, your heart rhythm becomes coherent and your sympathetic and parasympathetic nervous systems work in sync with one another. This coherence, or working together, translates to the brain with emotional well-being, reduced stress, and focused cognitive functioning. *This is why positive emotions feel*

so good. They actually cause harmony and balance to happen within your body's systems, so they aren't pushing against each other as they do when you are under stress or are experiencing negative emotions. (https://www.heartmath.org/science/)

There is a scientific principle called psychophysiological coherence. This is when the physical and mental and emotional parts of us are functioning with order and in harmony and balance with each other. Psychophysiological coherence is when everything is functioning at its best. Studies have shown that sustained positive emotions shift things within us, including the dialogue between the heart and the brain, to induce this state. As this happens, physiological entrainment occurs. This is when many bodily functions begin to synchronize with the balanced and harmonized and ordered rhythms of the heart. Everything works better. (McCraty, Rollin, Science of the Heart, Exploring the Role of the Heart in Human Performance Volume2, HeartMath Institite, 2015, Chapter 1, Heart-Brain Communication, www.heartmath.org)

As our heart and brain communicate in harmonious ways, the energy put out is calm and ordered and peaceful. Because our body is feeling the productive results as well, our thoughts and feelings tend to be more stable and tend to be more loving and kind and compassionate. As you can see, keeping sustained positive emotions in play is key. You can do this consciously and with intent. You can choose your emotions. Choose wisely. Choose love. Choose joy. Choose peace. Choose kindness. Choose compassion. Choose fun.

The HeartMath® Institute has been conducting current research

♥ *When you stay in a state of joy, internally everything works better. That then translates into the ability to more consciously connect to your intuitive gifts and the automatic connection you have when you interact with other life (people, animals, plants).*

on the connection between the heart and the brain, as well as other things. They have an online offering called <u>Science of the Heart</u> (McCraty, Rollin, Science of the Heart, Exploring the Role of the Heart in Human Performance Volume 2, HeartMath® Institute, 2015, Chapter 6, Energetic Communication, <u>www. heartmath.org</u>). They offer that the electromagnetic energy of the heart is much stronger than that of the brain and it extends several feet away from the body. The really interesting thing is that the person's emotional state is registered within that energy field. So, if you have two people interacting with each other the way we are used to thinking of communication, there is also an energetic communication happening simultaneously through the electromagnetic field. This also means that the principle of entrainment is in effect. That then means that the more aligned, balanced, and harmonized your body systems are, the more sensitive you may be to noticing this energetic connection. And, you may be able to positively impact the other person energetically.

♥ Breathe in love. Breathe in joy. Breathe in peace.

Note: The electromagnetic field of the heart can actually be measured by magnetocardiography. This type of measurement may be used at some point to evaluate the health of the heart. Pretty cool!

All this beautifully supports what I am sharing. Check out the HeartMath® Institute if you are interested in finding out more about the current science of how your heart and your body open you to, and support, your intuitive abilities, and how staying in a joyful state will actually help you be more intuitive. It is wonderful that studies are now able to publicly show this connection and they are being accepted (such studies have been going on for years and years but there were political and monetary issues that limited their impact and exposure).

* National Institute of Health - Cardiac Torsion and Electro-magnetic Fields -the Cardiac Bioinformation Hypothesis (https://www.ncbi.nlm.nih.gov/pubmed/15823696)

** APS - Easing the Heartache With Magnetic Fields - using magnetic fields to decrease blood pressure and improve heart health (https://www.aps.org/publications/apsnews/201705/magnetic.cfm)

Here are some related terms that will come in handy as you engage with the expansions in this book.

Breath

It is possible to re-pattern your heart rate with breath. That is why many meditative techniques incorporate deep rhythmic breathing. However, sustained positive emotions will do the same, without the focus on the breath, in my opinion. Perhaps as you are working toward a positive emotion when it seems challenging, some deep rhythmic breathing with an audible output would be helpful to set the pace and to allow you the energetic space to shift your emotion. As your emotions shift, your breathing will automatically synchronize and become more rhythmic and balanced with the heart.

Breathe in love. Breathe in joy. Breathe in peace. Allow those energies to flow from your heart throughout your body in full harmony and balance, synchronizing all systems as they flow and infusing them with the energies. Envision yourself as perfect, whole, and complete. Envision all of you – physical,

♥ *People feel your good thoughts and your not so good thoughts, even if not consciously. Practice noticing what you think and choosing love.*

mental, emotional, and spiritual working together in perfect concert – singing the song of you.

Biofields

As has been discussed, the heart has a strong electromagnetic field within which information about you is encoded and with which others can connect and receive. You can do the same with someone else. And, guess what! You do - all the time - though for many of you, it is not something of which you are consciously aware.

Your emotions and the emotions of the other person matter. They impact the type of connection, the strength of the connection, and the results of the connection. You can learn how to strengthen the energetic vibration of your heart, how to be consciously aware of doing that, and how to consciously and intentionally connect to someone else through the heart. Just remember, everyone - including animals - has a right to not be violated. Everyone has free will and deserves the right to choose with whom to connect, whether to connect, and when to connect – outside of automatic connection. Honor that as you learn and grow.

People feel your good thoughts and your not so good thoughts. Distance doesn't matter. Both positive and negative feelings and thoughts can be felt physically and emotionally by people who are sensitive to energy. And, even if someone cannot feel the energy you are putting out - yet - they are still impacted. If you are thinking (and I sincerely hope not!) "Yeah revenge!", just know that generating and harboring that type and level of negative energy hurts you a lot more than the other person,

♥ *You have light within your body. And external light impacts your body. What if you ARE Light and the internal light is just a connection to the totality that is you?*

on many levels. So, be careful what you think and feel about people. It is more powerful than you know, and it is a lot more impactful to you than you can imagine. If you must think through a challenging situation with someone, imagine the internal conversation held within an impenetrable bubble. Think your thoughts. Yell, scream, or whatever and then see the entire thing dissolve completely. Have it be your intention - even if you really don't want to - that the other person not be negatively impacted in any way. Remember, you are a creator. You are powerful. And so is your energy. Remember, too, that as you raise your own thinking and feeling to align with love and joy and peace, lower vibrational thinking and feeling is not sustainable and neither is the energy that brought in something less than optimal for you.

Biofields have also been photographed. Kirlian photography is able to capture the electrical corona discharge in picture format. Have you heard of aura photography? That's a more common name these days. The Kirlian process uses a specific technique. There are other types of cameras and processes that claim to capture the aura on film these days. Plants, animals, people… all have auras. Some people easily see them. Others can see them sometimes. All of us can be amazed when we look at the photos.

So, you've heard of bioluminescence I'm sure. Fireflies, or what I've always called lightning bugs, exhibit. Some sea creatures exhibit it. According to the National Institute of Health (NIH), the process occurs due to specific chemicals in an organism and it results in the emission of light from the organism. Biophoton(s), on the other hand, is a name for the photons of light within an organism and, according to the NIH, is not to

♥ *Let the Light of you dance with the Light of me. Let the Light of all kiss our hearts and fire our inner sparkle.*

be confused with bioluminescence. They are particles of light generated within the body and are radiated from the body. Just in case you wanted to know! It's all fascinating. That I know! And whether it relates to humans or not, I especially love seeing bioluminescence happening in organisms in the surf, like jellyfish. It makes nighttime wave watching so very joyful. And who doesn't love fireflies, both yellow and green? But, especially wonderful, is knowing that we, as humans, generate and radiate light too! Are you thinking what I'm thinking? I hope so! Let's make light and radiate it consciously! Fabulous!

* National Institute of Health - Biophotons as Subtle Energy Carriers; go to (https://www.ncbi.nlm.nih.gov/pmc/articles/PMC5433113/)

** National Institute of Health - non-invasive Bioluminescence Imaging used to study biological processes (https://www.ncbi.nlm.nih.gov/pmc/articles/PMC2713342/)

♥ *You are the Light of love.*

Light

Acupuncture has been around for a long time. It is thought that light flows through the body along the acupuncture meridians (kind of like a body superhighway for light). What if this light was, in fact, part of your soul essence that keeps you connected to your Source energy? And, what if it can be used for healing? And, what if you can learn how to "brighten" the light within you consciously?

There are mitochondria within each cell. They make ATP (adenosine triphosphate) which is our energy source. They also absorb light. Science has noted that when cells die, the light in the mitochondria diminishes – which you would expect as the development of ATP is not a stand-alone process. Therefore, when a person dies and their cells die, science has noted that the light within them dims and goes out.

The National Institute of Health (NIH) is exploring light therapy as a means of healing (photobiomodulation), and they are evaluating biophotons (light within the body) as a non-invasive way to detect serious health conditions. They have found that light impacts cellular functioning, including accelerated ATP functioning. So, if light is a factor in the making of the energy that keeps us alive, it follows (at least to me) that we do indeed have light within our bodies and that it plays a key factor in our health and well-being. If you can use light therapy to stimulate the mitochondria to make ATP and to increase the light within the body, why can't each of us learn how to brighten our inner light consciously? I believe we can. So how better to help others and ourselves than to "brighten our light". Perfect, right?

What if you envisioned light within every cell of your body with the intention that doing so will increase biophotons within the body? The NIH has published studies on this. Imagine the possibilities if we use this information consciously to increase the light within us and our connection to our Source energy. Meditation is a great way to do this.

To me, the light within our mitochondria is our <u>body</u> connection to our soul. I believe we are a "focused projection" of our soul. I believe each lifetime is a projection and they can be happening simultaneously. So, when the body connection dims, we "go within" or "go back" to that more expanded version of us. That

♥ *You, your soul, and your body could have so much fun making Light. Are you in?*

is why when people say, "the answer is within", I view that as turning our focus from the pinpoint that is our earthly life to the more expanded view which is "going back", or within, to our soul. That connection feels like an expansion (and it is from our current view), but it is really returning within the magnitude of our soul, which is also a part of the larger Divine Energy of Creation – the energy of all life everywhere, combined. To me, that makes the "as above, so below" and "as within, so without" make sense. We are never separate from our souls. Even when the body dies, we are good to go. We just are expanding into a more comprehensive and wholistic understanding of all that we are.

*National Institute of Health - Biophoton Detection and Low-Intensity Light Therapy (https://www.ncbi.nlm.nih.gov/pmc/articles/PMC2957070/)

** National Institute of Health - The Nuts and Bolts of Low-Level Laser Light Therapy (https://www.ncbi.nlm.nih.gov/pmc/articles/PMC3288797/)

*** National Institute of Health - The Use of Low Level Laser Therapy for Musculoskeletal Pain (https://www.ncbi.nlm.nih.gov/pmc/articles/PMC4743666/)

♥ *Just you being you makes the world brighter.*

Vibration and Frequency

Scientists can give you many definitions of vibration and frequency and wavelengths, but I would like to share my understanding of them from a spiritual perspective.

Everything is energy. Every energy has a vibration. There are many things that impact the level and frequency of a vibration. For cells in your body, your emotions and feelings and thoughts and expectations and patterns and desires and your overall health impact the vibratory rate of the cells. Scientists have found that when you are thinking and feeling and experiencing things that make you happy, your vibratory rate goes higher. The higher vibratory rates are also impacted by synchronicity and coherence of your bodily systems (alignment, harmonization, and balance). And those, in turn, are impacted by your emotional state, with those that are aligned with making you happy being ones that will bring you into a greater state of synchronicity and coherence. Therefore, *when you are happy, when you are experiencing and feeling love and joy and peace and your body is functioning more efficiently and effectively, your vibratory rate is going to rise and you are going to be better able to connect to the energy of your soul and to the energy of the Divine Energy of Creation.*

♥ *Your vibration holds the key to your pathway to your soul energy.*

So, when I say that something is going to raise your vibration, that's a really good thing! Your vibration holds the key to your pathway to your soul energy. Your soul energy is where you are able to access your intuitive gifts. And, it is from the energy of your soul, that you are able to understand that you are already enlightened. That's a no brainer to me! Are you in?

Oh, and did I mention that when you are in a state of love or joy or peace that your light *automatically* brightens because you become more coherent and synchronized, or what I call aligned and harmonized and balanced? Thus, your body works better, which includes that superhighway for light called the acupuncture meridians. And, all your chakras become clear and able to accept and channel your soul energy. Woohooscoobydo! I love that! So easy. Find what you love and do it, be aware of it as you're immersed in it, and give thanks. Easy, right?

Creating and Manifesting

What if there was another way to view creating your life and manifesting? What if the creating piece is the summoning of the energies required to put together what you desire? Manifesting is then the bringing of those summoned energies into the now.

I find that one of the biggest roadblocks to conscious creation is not knowing what you desire. For many, if you ask them what they want, they reply that they don't know. They may want a car, but don't know what kind. They may want a beautiful estate overlooking the ocean, but they can't describe it. It's more of a nebulous desire that is not fully formed. There is an underlying desire that has not yet been verbalized.

Forcing those desires doesn't bring the energetic properties to the table that will work best for you. It's almost akin to the energy of struggle. Yet, if you don't know, how do you get to where you do know without forcing yourself to choose something?

I have found that a wonderful and amazing way to address it is to look at the desired *outcome*. For most desires, the end result that is desired is safety, comfort, happiness, and/or love.

♥ *Sometimes we believe ourselves to be open and willing to allow – holding space – but the reality is that we are not there yet. The more you stay in a state of joy, the more that will automatically shift for you. So, what art makes you joyful? Go do some! And be mindful of it and in gratitude for it. It's not hard! Truly!*

Whenever you desire something, there is a reason that you desire it. And, the reason is not always obvious – well, at least the bottom-line reason.

Take the example of desiring a car. You would think it would be for transportation. Well yes. And… it also addresses the need for safety and providing for self and family, to name a couple of desired outcomes. That then leads to happiness and a more open heart with less stress and worry.

♥ Let your heart show you what you truly desire. Learn the language of your heart.

So, what if you aimed to uncover the bottom desired outcome first? What would happen if you then created the space (i.e. were open to and willing to allow) and summoned the energy for the most expanded and best way for you to have that desired outcome to arrive and serve you in the now? The Divine Energy of Creation (the energy of all life combined) has your back. This energy knows how to fully meet your needs in the most expanded and best way. Yet, we tend to want to control how this plays out. What if you chose to allow your most expanded expression of self – your soul – as part of and as the Divine Energy of Creation, to choose the best expression of your desire for you? What if you allowed your soul to summon the energy for it and then all you had to do was to embrace that gift of Spirit and allow it to manifest before you? It's possible and so very easy to do.

This way of understanding and embracing your ability to consciously create shifts the focus from what you don't have but want, to the energy of knowing your power as a Divine creator/co-creator. It is an empowering way of creating. Your brain may balk a little and say you are giving up "control", but how is having the illusion of control working for you right now? Believe it or not, empowering yourself in your realization and understanding that you are a part of, and you ARE, the Divine Energy of Creation is actually taking "control" as we have come to know it. It is in the embrace of (some will call it "surrender to", but I find that typically has a lot of attached non-serving beliefs) your Divine nature and stepping fully into that, that you evoke your own power and capabilities and beautiful spiritual gifts such as intuition.

You are here to create and enjoy what you create. You are fully capable of creating your life while honoring the rights of all others to choose their paths and options and creations. You have the right to do so. And, the Divine Energy of Creation is available for you to use to summon exactly what is needed to make it happen. Right now. Are you ready to play?

♥ One of the biggest roadblocks to conscious creation is not knowing what you desire.

Intuition

A lot has been written about the various types of intuition. Everyone wants to be intuitive. However, not everyone wants it for altruistic reasons. *The various types of intuition are gifts from your soul. They are glimpses into the "life" of your soul.* And, they can come in very handy!

We've all experienced a level of intuition from time to time, even if we didn't describe it as such. Remember the time the phone rang and it would be the person you were just thinking about? Or remember the time someone said something and your stomach immediately knotted up?

As you begin to live in the energy of love and joy and peace, you will find that your intuitive gifts automatically engage without any effort. Intuition also begins to open as you begin your spiritual journey and begin to try different techniques to quiet your mind and open your heart. Learning to reconnect to wonder and joy and awe and creativity, and through that avenue to your intuitive gifts, can be so much more fun and quick, though. It's your choice. Or, you could choose to pursue both (other techniques and reconnection) simultaneously.

Here is a little bonus that I learned, and it really helped me.

We all want to "see" things – clairvoyance. We want it to show up as a movie in our brains – and it may. But, for many, that's not how it displays. For me, when I would attempt to "see", I'd close my eyes and all I would see was black, the inside of my eyelids. Bah humbug! Until I got clarity.

So, if I asked you to go to your favorite grocery store and get a loaf of bread, you've already gone to the store and walked right to the place in the store where the bread lives - in your mind - haven't you? Of course you have! We do it all the time. Yet, we don't think of that as intuitive. But, that's the way many people "see" intuitively. It's exactly the same. It may get more vivid and shift as you practice and open to your intuitive gifts. That's normal with any learning. You build on what you already know. Everyone knows how to visualize already. You just may not have called it that. Visualization is part of clairvoyance – especially at the beginning.

♥ *Intuition is a glimpse into the "life" of your soul.*

That's your first step to opening to visualization which will help you in meditations and just connecting to the energy around you. If you close your eyes and intend for all the energy around you to "show" you, and then give it some time to do that, you may really enjoy the results! You've got to start somewhere. Another hint here… don't attempt to decorate it and embellish it. In other words, go with what you visualize and don't add to it if it doesn't immediately make sense. Just note it as it presents. That is all that is needed from you – just the intention to allow, and the desire. This is beginning to step into your power. Energy likes action! Have patience with yourself. You've got this. Be happy your intuition led you here now reading this so we can play with this together!

Another thing to do is to surround yourself with high-frequency music that makes you happy, art that makes you happy, colors that make you happy, and people who make you happy. Our fantastic amazing brains may begin to synchronize our brainwaves to the electrical charges and energy we are around. There is a scientific term for this. It's called the Frequency Following Response.

Our brains send out electrical charges in response to things we experience too! It's called the Cortical Evoked Response. That's why *being around positive people matters*. That's also how, if you are holding a vibration of love and joy, other people can benefit just by being around you! Cool, right? I love that!

♥ Being around positive people matters. YOU being positive around people matters.

Your brainwaves are generally associated with specific mental states. That's why so many are encouraging others to meditate. It helps you get in a brainwave that promotes relaxation, good feelings, and helps you to be able and willing to open to your intuitive gifts. Creating through art can do the same thing! So can being in a state of joy and love and peace. When your brainwaves synchronize and balance and are functioning harmoniously, the health benefits are tremendous! The exercises in this book are designed to assist you to do that in fun and enjoyable ways.

If you endeavor to be happy and surround yourself with happy positive people, the entrainment principle (physics) will come into play. All your cells will begin, with enough time, to entrain or synchronize with the vibration rate that is the "highest". There is music available now that has certain rhythms within it such that when you listen you will likely become relaxed and your creative state will likely open. You can find them by searching for binaural and monaural beats and/or isochronic tones. I have a lot of music of that type and I love it.

During meditation and certain healing techniques, the brain hemispheres synchronize and various parts of the brain work better together. It is pretty common knowledge now that the left side of the brain has been associated with logical and analytical thinking and the right side with artistic and creative talents and intuition. Can you imagine what would happen if both sides were working together? Well, you don't have to imagine anymore! You might say miracles. I would say it's your alignment to your greatness and who and what you really are. To be in such a state regularly - with intent - enhances your ability to access your intuitive gifts and provides you with a higher level of clarity and a more expanded truth.

♥ *Did you know that your energy directly impacts everyone with whom you come into contact? Knowing that, are you willing to be grumpy and have it potentially negatively impact someone else? Is that what you would consciously choose? Now that you know...*

If you think of it in terms of a radio antenna, it would be like fine-tuning it to receive the best quality signal. You become more able to receive intuitive information and to be aware of it when you do. You are then able to learn how to direct it for the desired results. Additionally, as you open spiritually and intend to stay in a high vibrational state, you begin to clear your energetic pathways. As those clear, you begin to experience your energy system functioning as it was originally intended.

This heightened state of vibration and synchronization has also been found to activate the left anterior portion of the brain - the portion of the brain associated with joy. This, in turn, promotes a strong immune system. It has been proven scientifically that sustained joyful and/or positive thoughts produce measurable positive physical differences. Because, as you are joyful and resonating at a high vibration, your body systems become aligned, balanced, and harmonized i.e. synchronized and coherent and, as such, they work together efficiently and effectively and easily for the best result.

You have an incredible energy system. It is typically called the chakra system. Each chakra can be a clear avenue for the giving and receiving of energy. The major and most well-known of the chakra points are said, by some, to relate to the endocrine system within the body. There are seven commonly accepted chakras. One is at the top of your head, the crown. One is between your eyes, the third eye. One is in the throat, the throat. One is in the heart, the heart. One is in the solar plexus or middle of your stomach, the solar plexus. One is in the lower abdomen, the sacral. And one is at the base of the spine, the root. You can find an incredible amount of information about the chakra system online. Some sources discuss many more chakra points. I have noticed energy not paying attention to the chakra system and just coming and going at will and wherever desired. But, it's good to have a place to start.

The thing to know for our purposes is that they exist. Each is associated with a part of being human such as fight or flight, love, expression, spiritual connection. When this system of energetic flow is functioning properly, your intuitive capabilities are naturally increased and your connection to the Divine Energy of Creation is clear and free-flowing. This results in good health and mental, emotional, and spiritual stability.

♥ *Beta, Alpha, Theta, Delta, Gamma – our brainwaves. Each is important. Yet, some are more supportive of intuition and spiritual development. I like Theta and Gamma. Breathe deeply and let your heart expand. Feel and know the love that you are. That will put you squarely where you want to be.*

Your beliefs, both conscious and subconscious, impact this flow of energy. For every stimulus you encounter, there are chemical and electrical impulses sent by the brain throughout your body. Your state of mind impacts this flow as well. When you live in a state of joy and with an awareness of life around you and your spiritual connection to it, any chakra issues can automatically resolve. That's what you want! You want to live in a state of love and attract only love and joy and peace and what comes from that. And, you want to believe and know and act on your ability to consciously create what you desire!

♥ *You've got this. Just relax and allow it all to sink in. Just by reading this, you are receiving. Cool, right?!*

Changing Beliefs and "Asking"

♥ What if beliefs, feelings, and patterns could auto-resolve for your best life?

You may be in a place in your life where you are thinking you'd like to connect to your spiritual side more fully, connect to your intuitive gifts, and be more present in life. But there's a problem, right? There is the time issue, the money issue, the "this" issue and the "that" issue. How could it ever work?

Well, Hello There! I am here to assist! You will notice that I have mentioned beliefs a lot. They're important! And, I've talked about how to have a conversation with yourself to get to the origin of the belief. Some of you, however, are still scratching your heads wondering what to do. How do you then change a belief?

I learned how to change beliefs by taking multiple classes and with a lot of self-help. I really didn't enjoy the accepted quintessential method of meditating. Sitting quietly while slowly and rhythmically breathing in and out with a candle burning and the lights low just wasn't my thing – and still isn't. So, I decided I would try another way.

I got comfy, opened a document on my computer, and said:

"OK God, tell me what I need to know." Well, at first that just didn't go anywhere very fast…or even at all. I realized I wasn't well versed enough in the class teachings yet to just "ask". So, I'd choose a belief to explore. For example, I might choose "I believe life is fun." I'd type that in and then wait to see what popped up in my mind related to that belief. With this example, it shifted into "I believe _____ is fun." If you were doing this, you'd then write down every thought about it that drifted in. As you practice, even just a little, this becomes really easy and will uncover some things that you would never have gotten to on your own. Don't worry if it makes sense or not. Just write whatever comes to you.

If there is something that you write down that doesn't suit you and you'd like to change it, explore how you came to have that belief. When did you first have the experience? Who was there? What did you think and do at the time? And keep going until you feel you have the answer. Then, intend and commit to forgiving yourself and everyone else involved and not having that belief rule you from now forward. Yes, they rule you. You know they do!

You can also use the same process for feelings. "I feel _____ about silly putty." or "Silly putty makes me feel _____." It's like being your own psychotherapist! Be honest! It's only you and the expanded you and the Divine Energy of Creation (and they already know the most expanded truth of it all!).

If it seems scary to figure out what you REALLY feel and who you really are, imagine support. Imagine a circle of beautiful shimmering angels around you and being there to hug you when

♥ *Make beliefs your friends. Allow them to alert you and teach you. Don't enshrine them. Allow them to free-flow. Teach beliefs what type you enjoy and what type you do not. They are fast learners and they love to be friends.*

you may need it. Or, you could imagine anything that would make you feel safe and loved and supported (like a roomful of puppies!). You already have the support. You are already loved. You are already safe. But, you may not always feel that and feel connected to all that. So, imagine it and allow your desire to become real in that moment. That, actually, is a type of meditation from a broad perspective. No need to feel silly. You are doing what the "experts" say is helpful and cathartic. Yea!

♥ Your beliefs are not who you are. They are simply beliefs and you can choose to change them. And, you can partner with them to create your best life ever!

That's one part of changing beliefs and asking. You did ask about the beliefs and then allowed the thoughts to come. What if you had a question? What if you wanted to know if you were making the right choice on something big in your life? Until those answers just flow to you because you desired them, you can use a "tool" that will work.

Go online or to the bookstore and purchase a book of spiritual quotations (see my favorites at the end of the book). Ask the question in your mind with the intention of getting an answer. Intend for something in the book to provide you with just the information you need to make the best choice and intend that you open the book to the perfect page for that and your eye be drawn to the exact spot for the answer. I think you will be amazed at how accurate and telling this little tool will be.

Another way to receive answers is to first ask and then allow the answer to come to you in a variety of ways. At first, this may require patience! We want our cookies NOW! Of course you do. But, assuming that you are not aligned and connected in a way to have your cookies just appear on a plate before you instantly - yet - allow the Divine the chance to line up things to bring you what you desire. You may have beliefs or feelings or patterns or resistance of a variety of types that require shifting before you will allow your creation. Anticipate the answer via a phone call, or a passage you read, or something someone says in passing, or a random thought, or... Answers can flow to you in a multitude of ways. Don't limit the opportunities. Be aware. Be expectant. Be patient. If you wait, they will come!

And finally, there is yet another way. The methods above are for those of you whose cookie monsters are howling. So, what is the other way? It's by taking the 101 days described in the second part of this book and following each day's recommendation with happiness (that you're taking the first step), expectation (that this might actually be fun AND work), and gratitude (for your spiritual team that has your back, wants the best for you, and loves you dearly). *I truly believe that as you raise your vibration and begin to see the beauty and wonder of life in a more expanded way and begin to be present and engage it (as a part of you), you will begin to live in the vibration of joy. As you do that, I believe beliefs and feelings and patterns will auto-resolve.* If you conscientiously, and with reverence, embark on this journey of self-discovery and self-mastery and self-love, things will just be. Things will just flow. You will notice synchronicities. You will notice that the world seems brighter and shinier and more sparkly. You will notice that you have forgotten to judge yourself or others. You will notice compassion and kindness in your words and actions. And you will come to a place of wonder and awe at all the spiritual gifts available to you every moment of every day. That's worth the risk, isn't it? Put on your hat and let's go explore!

♥ *Answers can flow to you in a multitude of ways. Don't limit the opportunities. Be aware. Be expectant. Be patient. If you wait, they will come!*

Time to Be Open

Is it ever not the time to be open? Just musing…

Every day on this journey, I'd like to encourage you to take a bit of time and intend to be open to all possibilities, all options, all points of view. I believe truth is on a continuum. I believe that where you "plug into" that continuum sets the framework for what you experience and what you come to believe. Given that, I believe all points of view to be true and, therefore, no one is wrong. However… the more expanded the view, the closer to the infinite truth of the Divine Energy of Creation – God, Allah, the Universe, Source, etc. (by any name or understanding).

♥ *Allow clarity, understanding, and truth to flow to you in unlimited ways.*

So, when you are plugged into only one point on the continuum and not recognizing that you are, in actuality, *all of them*, your vantage is not the most expanded and comprehensive. You can view it as if it were a radio. You can dial into a number of channels playing beautiful (mostly – haha) music. Or, you can turn it off and make your own music as you connect to all that is around you and within you.

You change where you are connected based on your openness to change and options, and your beliefs and thoughts and feelings. We tend to think in linear fashion. From that vantage, as you change your vibration and frequency to those more closely aligned with love and joy and peace, you "go higher" on the continuum. I don't like to view it from this vantage because we are hardwired to think "higher" is better than "lower". And, that's a kind of "yes and no" sort of thing. In any case, let's just go with it for the sake of understanding it in a simple manner.

What if today you just began the process of being open to something more comprehensive in truth than where you are now in your spiritual beliefs? What if you allowed that even though you truly believe what you believe, there might be more? What if you began to understand that if you hold on too rigidly to what you now believe, you are actually limiting your understanding of the most expanded truth of the Divine Energy of Creation?

So, be open. Be expectant. Allow understanding to come to you in multiple forms and via multiple methods. Don't limit how it comes. The energy held within a book... the energy of the bird as it flies and sees from a different vantage... the energy of the unconditional love of your pet... the energy of being drawn to a talk or writing of a new spiritual teacher... There are so many ways to allow. Just be aware. Look at everything as a potential teacher and messenger. If you don't immediately see the message or the teaching, that's just fine. Just being open to the possibility allows for understanding on some level of your Being. Conscious awareness will come. It doesn't have to be a process, but many are conditioned that a process is necessary. So, until that is cleared for you, go with it. Be thankful. Give thanks as you experience your day even if you are uncertain about what it is you are receiving. I would offer

♥ *What if you could view change like the sky when clouds roll by, or the change in trees during the seasons, or which birds come to visit today, or the expectation of something wonderful about to arrive? As we experience life, we sometimes begin to harden to change. We no longer want the unexpected. We no longer value change. I would offer that merely adjusting your perspective would offer you the opportunity to embrace positive change and learn from change you wouldn't consciously choose. Not all change is the same. Allow space for that. In doing so you take away the power of resistance to change.*

that it is generous, loving, expansive, joyful and that you are being assisted to become more consciously aware of being embraced by the Divine. How awesome is THAT?

The first step sets the outline of your path. You choose whether to follow the defined "trail" or whether to venture out on a path of your own. All eventually lead to all others. And the journey is as infinitely enjoyable as the outcome, if you allow it to be. So, on this journey, step out of your comfort zone and see where you are pointed. It's a glorious adventure of life. Become consciously involved. You'll be so happy you did!

♥ *What if you allowed that even though you truly believe what you believe, there might be more?*

Creative Expression Through Art and Why It Is So Important

Let's start at the beginning. What is art?

When you read a book and are really engaged, you are immersed in art. You are interpreting – creatively and artistically – the story presented by the author. You are the one who infuses meaning and life beyond the obvious. You are the one who "applies" it to your own understandings and perceptions and beliefs and feelings. You are artistically interpreting the author's presentation. That's creative. Bravo!

Everything is art. Why? Because you are painting the canvas of you and your experiences moment-to-moment. So, when you hug and love your dog, you are artistically breathing life into that moment, infusing custom feelings and custom understandings. You are reacting and responding artistically to all that happens moment-to-moment. That is art. You are an artist!

What if that art was inspired and "directed" by that most expanded part of you that we typically call the soul? What

♥ *You are painting the canvas of you and your experiences moment-to-moment. You are the artist, and you are the art!*

if that art was "created" by you, consciously, as the most expanded part of you rather than through the 3D mind? What do you believe your experience would be like? Do you think it possible that it could be anything other than joyful, love-filled, peaceful, amazing, awesome, inspired, creative, wonderful, brimming with possibilities, overflowing with prosperity of all types, and on and on? Would you like that in your life now?

This is you allowing YOU. This is you BEING YOU. You are so much more than what is identified by the senses. You can access that. Art, in a myriad of forms, helps to easily establish the pathway to that part of you. Be brave. Be bold. Be willing. And, take action. Just the act of attempting something that you are pretty sure you would love begins the process. It's not mysterious. It's not hard. It only takes you desiring to and then doing something with that intent as the foundation of it. Joy is the intent. Expressing joy through art is the intent. Allowing connection to the Divine Energy of Creation, consciously, is the intent. Don't overthink it. Just begin and follow what you feel and think in the moment, without the peanut gallery of thoughts critiquing you. Whatever you create is perfectly fine and wonderful. It's you saying to the Universe, "I want to connect to my own Divinity consciously." That, my friends, will get it done. Happy dance!

♥ Energy loves action. The dance of you is calling!

I'd love for you to join me on this epic journey to fully and consciously connect to your soul. From that space you can artistically create your life experiences moment-to-moment and access and BE all the majesty and glory and awesomeness and power and connectedness and clarity and truth of that. You can have that now. You can enjoy that now. You can create that now! Choice Point Creation Arts will show you how and you can take it from there. Bring out your inner artist and creator! Let that artist shine! Let that artist create moment-to-moment bringing you exactly what you desire to experience – artistically – with artistic strokes, with artistic experience, with artistic voice, with artistic passion, with artistic clarity and flow of the Divine within. You have a full palate. You have a complete orchestra. You have an entire workshop. You have a beautiful studio. You have it all. Use it to create YOU now! Enjoy!

♥ *The symphony of you is playing your love song. Are you listening or conducting?*

A Final Note Before We Begin

All artists and creators have times when the stroke committed in pen or paint or medium is not what they desired it to be. So, they improvise and use that "not seen as perfect" stroke as the basis for a more creative and individualized offering of the final art piece created. It's a really cool thing.

We are all so different (even though we may mask as the same), that there is always something somewhere that is exquisitely perfect for each one of us. It's the same with each of us. We are exquisitely perfect. Some will resonate with that variation, and some will not. And, that's the way it's designed to be.

You are the most amazing you ever. You are already enough. You are already perfect. You are already enlightened. All you need to do to live a joyful, full, abundant, and amazingly creative life is to reconnect to that. You can do that by reconnecting to wonder and awe and through coming to believe that you are the artist and creator of your life. Joy is yours for the taking. Wonderful abundance in all areas of your life is waiting for you. Love is everywhere and in everything. Open your eyes and heart to it all and live life joyously and prosperously and beautifully – just as you want – by design, your design. Ready, set, let's do this!

♥ *Each of us is exquisitely perfect. Right now!*

♥ *Even what we call imperfect is perfect! We create imperfection with our beliefs and feelings. Because, there really is no imperfection. We just believe it to be. We can change that!*

♥

Your choice.
Your design.
Your creation.
Your art.
Your life.
What's your pleasure today?

♥

Part Two

The Journey Begins

Let your inner sun shine!

First Expansion

First Expansion is designed to get you back in touch with childlike innocence, imagination and carefree abandon. Reconnecting you with your body, the earth, your essence - and fun is the goal.

Please note:

Don't take the fun out of being spiritual and don't think you have to in order to BE spiritual. You can be reverent and spiritual and have fun all at the same time. The Divine Energy of Creation does not restrict you on your journey. Only you do. Lighten up. Be happy. Be thankful. Dance. Sing. Play. Be you. It's all OK! The Divine Energy of Creation still loves me and gifted me the understanding of what I am sharing with you here, so it must be just fine to have fun and be joyful and yet still hold a space of reverence and endless gratitude for the Divine. Let's co-exist. And, let's have fun.

♥ *Dance! Sing! Laugh! Play! Enjoy! Give thanks!*

One further note, for the maximum benefit, **do only one expansion per day.** Really. The intent is to energetically instill whatever the exercise brings so that it will become a part of your conscious awareness. You are retraining your brain. You are rewiring your neural network. You are choosing to have all of you work together to support love and joy and peace. Give it the expansiveness to settle in. For many of you, this will be an unusual concept. But, if you're still reading, I trust completely that this is for you. Only one a day will keep the doctor away and reconnect you with play!

♥ Relax and enjoy the process. It's not a race. The more you can feel into the expansions each day and really experience them, feel them, enjoy them, and be thankful, the faster things will shift in a joyful way for you. Don't use 3D thinking. Use heart thinking.

Today I will enjoy a sunrise or sunset.

Reconnecting with the beauty of nature is a wonderful step to take toward happiness, joy, peace, and consciously creating your life. Nature is such a phenomenal gift of Spirit and spirit. It is easy to forget your cares and open your heart to a gorgeous sunrise and/or sunset. As you do this, get in touch with what it *feels* like. Feeling is key. What does it feel like to relax, sit back, and let nature entertain you and fill you with happiness and, hopefully, wonder and awe? Remember that feeling. We want to learn how to reconnect with that feeling anytime and anyplace. See, I told you this would be fun!

♥ *Follow the feeling to the pot of gold at the end of the rainbow.*

P.S. For those of you fortunate enough to see a sunset over the ocean, watch for the green blip as it finally seems to sink into the water. It's amazing!

Today I will appreciate a work of art.

I have come to understand and know that art is a beautiful, fun, and exhilarating pathway to your connection to the Divine Energy of Creation – the energy of all life combined. I have an expanded view of art. It encompasses a variety of avenues of expression and passion. I do not limit it to a painting on a wall. It can be nature in action. It can be the beautiful preparation and presentation of food. It can be an athlete embracing the body as a tool of expression. *Art is unlimited in presentation and form.*

♥ *Art is unlimited in presentation and form.*

What type of art do you love? Today, find a work of art and *really look at it. Feel it within you.* How does your body respond to it? What are you thinking as you view it? Give it your full and undivided attention. Appreciate the work, appreciate the artist, and appreciate your ability to enjoy it and where it "takes you". Remember the feeling. Art can easily connect you to the Divine.

Are you ready to use art as your partner?

Today I will do something creative.

Today is a great day to be creative! Every day is!

When I say that, where does your mind go? For some (perhaps many) of you it will go to "I'm not creative." or "I don't paint." or whatever version of that is yours.

Be creative in how you think about creativity! Cooking can be creative. Meditating can be creative. Gardening can be creative. Thinking can be creative. And there are always the staples of art, dance, song, and crafts.

Creativity is present in whatever makes your heart sing. It is present when you completely lose track of time while you are immersed in the activity. It is when you are present with the Divine life-force and you are sharing. It can be who and what you are in the here and now - every minute!

♥ *Let the artist in you recognize that you are the art of life.*

♥ *Be creative in how you think about creativity!*

You are a creative energy already. But, many have lost touch with that. However, you can reconnect to that beautiful amazing inspiring part of you. When you are joyful and ready, it just flows in. How many writers say they just write down what comes to them? How many musicians say the inspirations just immerse them within the music and they just follow the flow? How many painters allow the brushes and paints to define the vision they carry? I can tell you! Lots of them! Inspiration and a clear vision of the creative activity just comes to them - like magic! You have that potential even if you don't remember that yet.

Having the desire to be creative and in conscious connection with the Divine Energy of Creation will help you to allow it to flow – both the creative inspiration and vision, and the intuitive gifts of Spirit. But, energy likes action. Have the desire AND do something. It doesn't matter if what you accomplish and create is museum or concert hall ready. It's how YOU think and feel about it. It's all about you.

♥ Creativity is your soul singing a sweet song to you.

♥ Are you ready for your creativity to joyfully dance with you, sing with you, and rejoice with you? If not, ask yourself why.

When you open your heart to the possibilities of you being a creator of beauty and art, you open to the allowance of what already is. You set the stage for beautiful expressions of you to emerge and be seen by all. That's scary for some; cathartic for others. It can be your pathway to your own unique and amazing and valuable and valued intuitive gifts. And, the more you allow the flow of your creative nature, the more you open to your intuitive gifts – because on some level they are one and the same.

So today, be bold and be beautiful. And have that flow of you express itself some wonderful way in the here and now. Don't limit or confine how it must show up. Just allow what comes to you to be heard and embraced, and then follow through. There are no boxes to stay within. There are no lines to connect. It's just you connecting to a more expanded part of you and allowing that connection to merge you with the Energy of All. From there, everything seems like a miracle. From there, inspiration and ideas and expression joyfully dance with you, sing with you, rejoice with you. Really! And, that joy then flows through you and from you into your creative work. Have fun today! As you reconnect to your innate creative nature and the flow of it, you also reconnect to your understanding that you are the creator and artist of your life. That's right - you.

Today I will notice color.

How much time do you spend thinking about color? Color is such an incredible gift! From the most delicate pastels to the most bold primaries, color touches not only our hearts but our brains. Colors evoke associations. Associations evoke feelings. Feelings evoke emotions. And, that is the fuel of creating.

Nature is one of the best ways to appreciate color. Nature doesn't care one bit about red and purple being together or about using the color wheel. She combines all types of colors together for stunning displays. Those displays can inspire and intrigue and move you. Doesn't it seem like paying attention to color would be important?

For today, choose a color - any one you please. As you go about your day, look for that color. Seek it out. Wear that color if you have it in your closet. Try to imagine what that color feels like. Really! What would yellow feel like? Warm? Friendly? Nurturing? What would brown feel like? Solid? Masculine? Textured? Have you ever thought about how colors might feel? Most likely you have not. So, today is your day! Have fun with color. Allow it to cause you to smile. It certainly will if you allow that! Enjoy!

♥ *Colors evoke associations. Associations evoke feelings. Feelings evoke emotions. And, that is the fuel of creating.*

Today I will take a walk outside.

Nature is one of the very best neutralizers. When you've had a disappointment or something just isn't working, go outside and take a walk in nature. Plants have a very high vibration. They lovingly offer assistance when you need an energetic reboot. There is infinite variety, and it is exquisite.

♥ Take a walk on the wild side of nature! Happy happy, joy joy!

Really see what you are surrounded by. Feel the energy of the plants surrounding you and nourishing you. Sit quietly for a moment and breathe in deeply. Let your heart fill with gratitude that you have such a magnificent resource so readily available and that the plants are so willing to serve. Allow your out-breath to carry away any cares you may have.

By the way, have this walk be a device-free zone. You cannot be fully present and connect to what is available for you if your focus is divided. You will be thankful that you decided to give this gift to yourself.

Today I will sit in the sun.

There is something very comforting and nurturing that happens when you feel the warmth and see the brightness of the sun. You are receiving Vitamin D when the sun hits your bare skin. It is the best way to obtain this vital vitamin. The light also impacts various rhythms and patterns within your body. And the warmth is reminiscent of being held in love by another. *Let the light of the sun brighten your light and let the warmth of the sun warm your heart.*

Remember that within the mitochondria of every cell in your body is a speck of actual light? The biophotons. Remember that scientists have proven that when a person is dying, the light within each cell begins to dim. Imagine what impact consciously brightening your inner light will have on how you feel and how supportive it will be for vibrant radiant health.

♥ *Let the light of the sun brighten your light and let the warmth of the sun warm your heart.*

Envision the "Light" (Divine Light) within each cell brightening as you allow the sunlight to flow to and from your heart. See each cell become so bright that you see no darkened space between them. You see only Light. Let your inner Light glow! Then radiate that Light - your Light - out from your heart to the beautiful generous loving plants surrounding you, in gratitude for their service.

And if that wasn't enough(!), a wonderful friend of mine wanted to share her "sun meditation" with you. Here are her words. "Close your eyes for a few minutes and look up at the sun and allow the warmth to kiss your face as it does a big bright yellow sunflower. Experience the colors of red, orange and gold light through closed eyelids as it replenishes your inner power and refuels your zest for a joy-filled life of exploration of new experiences." How beautiful! Thank you, dear friend. What a treat and how easy and simple and powerful!

♥ *Let my inner sun and your inner sun connect in the dance of life.*

Today I will laugh out loud.

I'm sure you've heard the old adage "Laughter is the best Medicine." (Norman Cousins - <u>Anatomy of an Illness</u>) It's stood the test of time for a reason. Laugh. If you search for the health benefits of laughter, you will find many. Plus, it's fun! It just immediately makes you feel better.

As adults, many people have forgotten how to laugh. They smile or do a truncated version of a laugh. Have you heard an adult giggle lately? Think of "delight" or "glee". What feelings does that bring up for you? Are you tempted to laugh? When was the last time you had a good belly laugh? Laughter is good for the soul.

What makes you laugh out loud? If you don't know anymore, you have some homework to do!

♥ *Hehehe! Hahaha! Hohoho! A laugh a day will keep the doctor away!*

Today I will internally listen to a happy song throughout the day and feel its message as I go about my business.

Sometimes we have moments. Sometimes we just aren't feeling happy about our day to come. For those times, having a "go-to" or default "happy song" can make a huge difference.

In your head, play that song and feel its intended mood as you sit through yet another boring business meeting or as you wash all those dishes. Allow the music *and the feeling* of the music to move your attitude from complacency to happiness, from sadness to happiness, from blah to happiness.* It works and it's very easy. You can train your brain to know that when you think of that song and "play" it in your head that your intention is to shift into happiness – and quickly. Easy. Effective. Fun. Happy listening and happy feelings. Happy day.

♥ *What is your happy song?*

*Remember the list of emotions in the "What is Healing" chapter? Allow music to help you move up the list to love and joy and peace and happiness.

Today I will hum.

Many adults bury their desire to belt out a song. There are the excuses of "I can't carry a tune." or "I'm not good enough to sing in the company of others." Whatever the reason, it would be good and fun to change that! So today, hum. It's a baby step to get you "seasoned" for the next step which is to sing.

♥ *Do hummingbirds hum? Hhhmmm… just wondering.*

Today I will sing.

Sound is a fabulous way to recognize vibration and frequency. Music can bring on any mood; it can elicit any emotion. Think of how many times hearing a song has immediately taken you to a great memory. Think of the times when music has lifted your spirit. Science has even proven that plants react positively or negatively to sound. Schoolkids even do experiments to show that. It's powerful. So is the sweet sound of your voice. Whether you can carry a tune or even know what pitch is about doesn't matter.

♥ *Sing a siren song to your soul.*

Singing is good for the soul. It connects you with your body. It is you calling out to your soul. Allow yourself to imagine that as you sing. Imagine that you are singing a siren song to your soul to invite your soul into the here and now more fully as a partner and creator of your life. If you know you will judge yourself because you "know you can't sing" … stop it. Just jump in for a little time today and sing a little tune. Find a song that you love. Sing along with the radio. Sing in the shower where no one will hear. You are training yourself to re-discover the truth of who and what you are and to then embrace that truth for positive change and joyful creating.

Today I will make up a song and sing it out loud.

Song reconnects you with your soul, with what you desire – even if you don't consciously know what that is yet. Uplifting song is a way to allow yourself the freedom and space to take a look at who and what you are. With song that is not written by you, you have the feeling that if the message gets too close you can "deny" it, you can walk away. So, it feels safe.

Many songs are written from the heart by singer/songwriters. They take their own experiences and translate them into the universal language of music and song. As you listen, whether you realize it or not, you may be living vicariously through their words. Their words may be giving you voice where you didn't feel you had any before. The rhythm and the melody make it easy to connect to and make messages palatable where they might not have been before.

♥ *Let the sweet sound of your voice play the sweet sound of you.*

So, make up a little tune and sing it for two minutes. Don't leave me now! You can do this and it's vitally important. Set it to music you already know if that feels more comfortable. Make the song about how you are feeling about something. It doesn't need to rhyme or even make sense to anyone other than you. If you feel that you can't carry a tune, don't worry. This is just for you. You are not auditioning, except with your soul. Sing in the shower, sing in the woods, sing in the closet if you must – but sing – and out loud. That's right. Out loud. Your voice is powerful. Your voice needs expression. Your voice needs to be heard by you. Now.

Today I will go outside and jump for joy.

As adults, we can easily get into the habit of limiting our expression of joy and happiness. We save it for special occasions. We don't want to appear flighty or naïve. We want sophistication and we want respect. But, what if the paradigm of what is respectable is shifting to honor authenticity? What if honoring how you feel is worthy of respect vs. hiding your true feelings?

Jumping for joy will connect you to your body. Your body is a superb vessel. When you are connected to it, how you feel at any given moment is easy to detect. That, in turn, helps you to locate areas of your life that cause stress or discomfort or fear. Recognition is the first thing that happens before change. You will also begin to remember how much more vivid the world seems when you are fully present and engaged. Additionally, the action of jumping and then connecting with the earth reminds you, on a fundamental level, that you are supported. Plus, it's fun once you get over the shock of doing it as an adult!

♥ *Let your inner wild child shine!*

Today I will skip with abandon.

Have you ever skipped? It is such a joyous playful light-hearted energy! For an adult, it says "I don't care how it looks or how it is perceived. I am loving me and having fun with childlike wonder and expansive expression." The energy of that is two-fold. First, it gets you immediately to the energy and expectation of fun. Second, it allows you the freedom to feel what you feel and choose what you choose without the fear of judgment.

We tend to get bogged down with feelings that are concerned about how we appear to others. Those feelings have a base of fear – the fear of not being loved and accepted. Skipping today will allow you to reconnect to a time when you didn't even have the experience of knowing judgment. You just did things as it suited you to do them. This helps you to release guilt and release shame and allow what you truly feel to surface. For many of you, you won't even remember what it feels like to really be you. You are amazing just as you are. Let's reconnect with that.

♥ *Feel what you feel and choose what you choose without the fear of judgment.*

Today I am free to act like a joyful carefree child.

Are you ever closer to the Divine Energy of Creation (God, Allah, the Universe, etc.) than when you are in awe and wonder? Perhaps not. The exhilaration that comes from wonder and awe is something we tend to forget with time. Life gets in the way. Responsibility gets in the way. For today, find ways to re-capture and re-experience that joyful carefree childlike space. Perhaps it comes with skipping your way to the lunchroom and giggling at the looks from your co-workers. Perhaps it's buying a bubble wand and making bubbles. Perhaps it's blowing the seeds off a dandelion stalk (one of my favorites!). Perhaps it's chasing your dog. Find what is fun and delightful and childlike for you and do it. You will be so glad you did!

♥ *Reconnect to childlike wonder and expansive expression. It's who you are.*

Your cells have memory. They will remember the autonomic processes that happen from that level of joy and spontaneity. And, the more you practice finding that energy, the more your cells will seek it out. The more they will urge you to make it happen again. Your body is alive and more of a partner than you may realize. Help all levels of you to enjoy and love life even more. Joyful carefree childlike play will do that and do it quickly. Are you in?

Today I will dance with abandon for two minutes.

Dance connects us with both the here and now and our creative nature. As people age, many take on feelings of self-consciousness… feeling like what others think of their dancing is important to the level that how one dances, or if, changes.

We want to change that. We want to reconnect to childlike abandon. We want to free-flow creativity from the Divine Energy of Creation as we connect to the very instinctual rhythms of music. Just do it. Don't think about it. Don't figure out a sequence of steps. Just allow the music to show you. Allow the music to move you. Allow yourself the distinct pleasure of partnership with music.

The two minutes is a minimum. It is for those of you who feel like you can't dance, or you feel self-conscious dancing. For two minutes, just let that go. Dance through your home. Dance in the shower. Dance in the street. Dance anywhere. It doesn't have to be a dance you or anyone else knows. Make it up. For two minutes just be you, uninterrupted, untethered, free. Try it. I bet you'll like it.

♥ *Play! Play! And more Play!*

Today I will find something that smells wonderful to me and inhale it deeply. I will remember the smell and how it made me feel throughout the day.

Scientists have proven that smell has direct access to the brain. It can evoke strong feelings that may not even seem related. That's because it touches memories, even long-ago memories. What do you think of when you walk into a home and smell cookies (besides eating them immediately!)? There is a reason realtors bake cookies for open houses. It sparks memories of love, of caring, of home cooking, of home… A smell can take you right back to the emotions and feelings of when that smell was cataloged in your brain. Your brain responds to scent more quickly than to sight or sound. The way the nose and brain work together is through the Olfactory system.

♥ *Your brain is working to communicate with you. Be aware of what you feel and why you feel it.*

You can alter your mood just with smell. You can shift your alertness with smell. You can initiate healing with smell. What smells really good to you? As you smell it, be aware of the feelings it generates within you. What are those feelings? Can you identify them? That's especially important if there is a smell you hate.

My own story with smell involves the smell of liver. I was a young girl and my Mom cooked liver for dinner. I hated liver. Needless to say, it didn't go well. Even though I have cleared the trauma of that, I still dislike the smell of liver. Smell is powerful. Used appropriately, it can be very healing and soothing. Find what works for you and explore those smells that you hate and use them as springboards for understanding and healing.

Smell is a strong reminder. Smell can immediately take you back to so many things that you experienced but may no longer consciously remember. Given that, can you see how smells and understanding the origin of those smells have the capacity to heal the physical and emotional and thus raise your individual frequency?

Research is currently being done to explore the vibratory frequency of certain essential oils. They are finding that some have a very high frequency. That frequency, given enough time (which varies given a variety of factors), has the capacity to entrain the cells of your body to vibrate at a like frequency or, at the very least, a higher vibratory rate than you began with. Entrainment is the scientific principle that says that cells will begin to vibrate in resonance with the highest vibratory rate to which they are exposed, given enough time.

It will serve you to become aware of smells and how they make you feel. Explore different smells. Your brain is working to communicate with you. Extend a hand (or nose!) and work together for your best life.

♥ *When you are breathing deeply to harmonize and synchronize within your body, try inhaling the smell of something you love. Essential oils are great for this purpose! Rose… Frankincense… Go for one that you really love because that will be the one you need. Interesting how that works!*

Today I will find something that feels really good and I will caress it.

Have you spotted a trend here? We are working to engage the senses in a way that centers you in the here and now and is offering a refresher course to the brain to engage with the seemingly ordinary. There can be great joy and healing with that.

So, find a piece of cloth that is silky and smooth, or a plant leaf that delights you, or a lotion that feels creamy and luscious… whatever will touch feelings within you. I want to get you to a place where everything has the potential to do that for you. You begin with the first step. What do you feel within your body as you caress the thing you chose? What do you instantly think? Are the feelings good, or is there something else too? Enjoy the process. We'll revisit this again.

♥ *One way your brain communicates with you is via the senses.*

Today I will enjoy the taste of something very delicious.

We have been exploring the senses. Today it is taste. So often when we are eating or drinking something delicious, we aren't taking the time to really savor it, explore it, and appreciate it. We are talking to friends, reading our messages, watching television, or doing other activities. We aren't giving our experience the full measure of attention that it merits.

Today, find something that is yummy to you - either food or drink. As you partake, smell it. What is its texture? Allow it to dance with your taste buds. Consider the pleasure it is bringing you. What does that feel like? Does it bring up associated memories?

Today is a day I bet you will enjoy!

♥ *Given all the pleasure it brings, I bet the sense of taste is not something you consciously think about often. Do you take it for granted?*

Today I will appreciate nature in all forms.

Nature is amazing! Just being in nature can shift your vibrational frequency. *The beautiful rhythms of nature can calm your soul and gently remind you that you are eternal.*

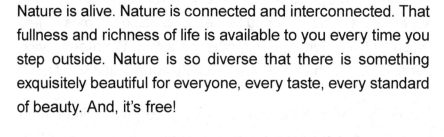

♥ *The beautiful rhythms of nature can calm your soul and gently remind you that you are eternal.*

♥ *Nature is so diverse that there is something exquisitely beautiful for everyone, every taste, every standard of beauty. And, it's free!*

♥ *Flying flowers... aaahhhhh. Love that!*

Nature is alive. Nature is connected and interconnected. That fullness and richness of life is available to you every time you step outside. Nature is so diverse that there is something exquisitely beautiful for everyone, every taste, every standard of beauty. And, it's free!

Look around you. Be grateful that the plants support your life. Be grateful that such beauty is everywhere. Be grateful that it all works together to offer what you experience. Notice the unfurling of a fern. See the beautiful striations of a rock formation. Smell the dirt after a gentle rain. Enjoy the flying flowers otherwise known as butterflies. * There are infinite opportunities to appreciate the gifts offered to you by nature. Take the time today to pause and notice... and give thanks for each one.

* Nod to Robert A. Heinlein for the beautiful visual!

Today I will be kind to all life.

Kindness is a special virtue. Kindness resonates within you in like measure to the kindness extended.

Kindness is defined by Wikipedia as "…a behavior marked by ethical characteristics, a pleasant disposition, and concern and consideration for others. It is considered a virtue and is recognized as a value in many cultures and religions."

When you are kind, you are training your brain to value others. You are training your brain to default to compassion and consideration – to put yourself in another's shoes and to treat that person (or animal) as if he or she is you. For, in fact, at the most expanded level of your being, you are part of the Divine Energy of Creation. That energy is the energy of all of us as One energy. You are a part of that, and you ARE that. So, the underlying impact is that you are helping yourself remember your own Divinity and all the spiritual gifts that arise from that. Kindness matters. Kindness helps the giver as much (and perhaps even more) than the receiver. What better way to love yourself than to be kind to others!

♥ When you are kind to another, you are loving yourself.

Today I will do something special for an animal.

Historically, humans have had a special bond with animals. Animals have served humanity throughout the ages in a variety of ways. Yet, for most of you reading this, your dependence on animals has changed. It's more choice based now and not "opted-in" out of necessity.

Honoring and respecting and valuing animals can not only bring you joy, it can also open your heart to the connection you have with all life. As part of the Divine Energy of Creation, you are part of all life everywhere. That includes animals and plants. The more you can connect with that truth, the more you will come to understand your place in the big scheme of things and your part of the whole of creation. As you do that, your intuitive abilities will begin to unmask. You will open to compassion and kindness and the value of all. As you value all, you also value yourself. That opens your gifts even more.

So, choose an animal and do something special for it today. Perhaps it's a bird outside your window that would love some birdseed that you could provide. Perhaps it's the spider in your home that you scoop in a cup and transport outside (insects count too!). Perhaps it's offering to do an hour of volunteer work at an animal rescue group. Perhaps it's walking a disabled neighbor's dog (a win-win-win as you also help the person and yourself). Be creative. I know you have it in you! And remember, feelings are the fuel for manifestation. The more you can truly feel the love and kindness you are sharing, the more you are telling the Universe "I want more of this". Now go love and create.

♥ *Animals are special gifts.*

♥ *Can you imagine what the world would be like without birds, for example? Mind blowingingly sad in my opinion! You've got your jazz birds, your opera birds, your cat call birds, your sweet melody birds… so many kinds and they all blend together in perfect harmony! I don't know about you, but they bring me GREAT joy. Let's respect and honor and value animals. They deserve it. You deserve it!*

Today I will do myself a favor.

We tend to think of favors as something we do for someone else with an unstated implication that something of like value will be reciprocated at some time. What if you came to understand doing a favor as an unselfish act of kindness and love with no future expectations, implied or otherwise, attached? The energy of that is of a much higher vibration and frequency.

Living in a high vibration will spark wonderful shifts and changes that you can't even imagine. Synchronicities will flow and be an everyday occurrence. Gratitude will become your middle name. What we call miracles, but are actually you fully connected to your Source energy and the results of that, will be showing up all around you. And, it will be wonderful.

♥ I love me "just because".

♥ Loving yourself puts you directly on the path of reconnection to wonder and awe.

So, do yourself a favor and love yourself enough to be present and do something worthwhile for yourself, without calculating the risk/reward value… just allow yourself to know what you would *value and treasure* (perhaps buy yourself a beautiful bouquet of flowers; perhaps go to a show; perhaps take the time to go for a swim; perhaps do that art that you never seem to have time for; perhaps visit a friend; perhaps eat cake!) and do that out of love for yourself (vs. feeling you deserve it because of something you've done or plan to do). Let today be a "just because…" day.

Today I will do something wonderful that nourishes me.

Many people think self-care is either selfish and/or unnecessary. It is neither. Self-care, and in this case doing something wonderful for yourself, is an expression of self-honor, self-value, self-respect, and self-love. All these attributes are valuable to assist you in allowing the flow of your own Divinity in the here and now. Allowing that flow will assist you in consciously choosing what you want to create in your life. I'd say that's worth doing something wonderful for yourself! Another win-win!

♥ *Self-honor. Self-value. Self-respect. Self-love. Yes. Yes. Yes. YES!*

♥ *Have you hugged yourself today?*

Today I will write down three things that make me smile. I will experience one of them.

Smiles are love letters to your heart. What better way to set your intention for the day than to express love to you. There are a multitude of wonderful healthy and emotionally valuable physiological impacts that occur from the action of smiling – especially when coupled with the feeling that you'd expect a smile to generate. Why not love yourself enough to give that gift to yourself today. I'm all for it! Smile and watch the world smile with you.

♥ *Smiles are love letters to your heart.*

Today I will be grateful for me.

We are taught from an early age that to be humble is a good thing. We may not always listen, but we are taught that! We are taught to be grateful for what others offer. But, I cannot remember one single time when I was taught to be grateful for me.

I have value. I have many things to offer and I am grateful that I exist. We tend to repress a lot of feelings because many of us are not taught how to deal with feelings – especially seemingly negative ones. Some of us allow others to tell us how to think and feel and act. Who we are as an individual can get hidden to the point that we don't even know who we are anymore.

♥ *Own you. Stand up for you. Enjoy you! And love you.*

The way to begin is to think about what you love. What do you love to do? What makes your heart sing? What makes time stand still? Then, explore deeper. Why do you get those feelings with those activities? You are uncovering you. Then, look at that person – the one that is feeling so amazing and doing wonderful things and who is so happy and joyful. Be grateful for that person. That person is you. Own you. Stand up for you. Enjoy you! And love you. That will have gratitude for you bubbling up like a lively stream. Allow those feelings to flow to every cell in your body. Remember what that feels like. When you feel anything other than joy and love and peace, bring back that feeling of gratitude for you. You deserve to be loved – by self and others. I don't care what you've done or how you believe you are perceived. You deserve to be loved and you deserve to love and honor and respect yourself. You are Divine. How could you not be worthy? You are a Divine

Being having a human experience. It's simple. I am grateful for you. You be grateful for you.

When you can be grateful for you, easily and effortlessly, you will find you are naturally and effortlessly grateful for all life. It's just what is. It's who and what you are. It's who and what all life is – a representation of the Divine on some level. You recognize that kindred energy and are grateful. You are not alone. Everyone is here for you. And, you are here for everyone. How amazing is that?

♥ *You are not alone. Everyone is here for you. And, you are here for everyone. How amazing is that?*

♥ *When you can be grateful for you, easily and effortlessly, you will find you are naturally and effortlessly grateful for all life. It's just what is.*

Today I will breathe consciously and deeply all day.

Consciously breathing deeply has many great health benefits. Who knew? It's why many meditations begin with several deep breaths and some meditative techniques focus on the breath.

Deep breathing helps to align, harmonize, and balance the various systems that are operating all the time in your body. Scientists call this synchronization and coherence. It's a good thing! As your systems align, balance, and harmonize, they communicate more effectively and efficiently. They work together in a more organized way. All this leads to less stress, better functioning, and increased mental clarity. All that opens the pathway to a deeper spiritual connection, which is what you want if your goal is to open to your intuitive gifts.

♥ Breath can give, expand, and take life. Breath is a wonderful partner.

So, today breathe consciously and deeply. Feel the changes in your body as you do. When you become consciously aware of how you feel related to what you choose, you are training your brain to know that you desire this feeling and you want more, even from other avenues of experience.

Pause. Breathe. Allow. Relax. Feel. Breathe. Easy.

Today I will be mindful of my body.

You've heard it said that your body is a temple. Whether you believe that or not, your body is amazing! There are so many independent systems and parts that work together seamlessly. You are able to explore this life and this world in the way that you do because of your body.

Your body is also wired to alert you when things aren't working. And that alert isn't just for the physical. It is also an alert for non-serving beliefs and patterns. When your body believes you to be living and acting authentically in all areas, the chemical and hormonal messengers easily flow and deliver their assigned task. However, if the body believes there is internal conflict or distress, those same messengers can back up and not flow. When that happens, a physical ailment occurs to alert you.

♥ *Your body loves you and wants to assist you in every way. Be a good partner to your body.*

For example, if you have a knee issue, ask yourself where in your life you may not want to move forward. If you have a cough or sore throat, ask yourself where you are not speaking your truth. There are books that can help you understand where to look for various ailments if that doesn't come naturally for you (an online search will reveal many).

The point is, however, to be mindful of your body and what it may be attempting to alert you to. How do you feel when you say things? How do you feel about the choices you make? Do you recognize when your body is getting tired – before you become exhausted? What is your body telling you throughout the day?

Believe it or not, physical ailments can be healed or shifted by changing beliefs and feelings. For example, you may have conflicting beliefs. You may hold both the belief "I love myself" and the belief "I hate myself". Those two beliefs do not play nicely together! They cause distress. You may feel very tired for no apparent reason. You may have stomach issues that are undefined. But, if you change the "I hate myself" belief, all that may instantly change (if that was the core cause of the distress). Cancer has been shifted by dealing with deeply held anger. It's more involved than I think you need here, but do be aware that your body is an "early warning system" for how you are thinking and believing and feeling. You can learn techniques and skill sets that will allow you to change non-serving beliefs instantly (or you can align with your soul such that they auto-resolve!). But first, you will want to become aware that your body loves you and wants to assist you in every way.

Are you ready to partner with your body instead of just going along for the ride?

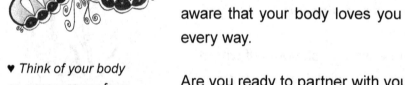

♥ *Think of your body as a messenger from your soul. Listen. Feel. Appreciate. Be mindful.*

Today I will shine my inner sun all day.

This is such an amazingly fun thing to do. Just imagine that your heart is the sun. Imagine your inner sun shining brilliantly. Imagine that the energy of your inner sun fills your body and the rays of your inner sun extend from your body until you and your inner sun are One. Throughout the day, allow your inner sun to smile at everything, especially people. Allow it to send beautiful bright brilliant energy to everything. Enjoy your little secret – spreading sunshine and cheer. And, remember... that light and brilliance is already within you and is you. You can make such a difference in the world just by shining your inner sun and enjoying doing it. Shine on!

♥ *Let your inner sun shine, Sunshine!*

Today I will surprise someone in a good way.

Helping others is a wonderful tonic for the soul. When you go out of your way to do something unexpected and nice for someone else with no expectation of reward (except inner happiness), you are eliciting the concept of altruism. You are opening neural pathways in the brain to consider the situation and feelings of others and then to consciously act to support their success and happiness. That, in turn, raises your vibration which, in turn, attracts an equal positive energy to you. Win-win!

♥ *Helping others is a wonderful tonic for the soul.*

Today I will reach out to a friend.

As humans, we are wired to want to communicate and share with someone else. It goes way back to a time when we more directly needed others to survive.

As we get busy with life and work and family, we may let some friendships slide. We still care about others, but we have responsibilities and demands and they must come first, we believe.

Today is about remembering what it is like to talk to someone you care about simply for the joy of it, with no agenda or feeling of obligation or guilt. It is about remembering that it is important to have and nourish friendships.

♥ Friends come in all shapes, sizes, temperaments, activity levels, and such. Isn't that fun? Have many or have a few. It's up to you. But, make them count.

Energetically, this helps to harmonize and balance your energy. Friendships are good for the soul. And, if you surround yourself with others who live in a space of love and joy and peace, that energy will automatically entrain any lower vibrating cells to vibrate at the higher resonance, given enough time. In other words, being around happy loving people will energetically be good for you!

Today I will make a difference to someone.

Altruism. Selfless concern for others. When you make a difference to someone, you are showing that you care. You are validating the person. As long as your thoughts and feelings don't go to the dark side and cause you to think you are better than another, your efforts will benefit both the other person and you.

Think about it. How would it feel to have someone validate you as a person, for no apparent reason, *just because you exist*? It would make you feel awesome, wouldn't it? I bet it would! So, imagine what the person you choose will feel. Probably the same, even if they can't put words around it. It will open your heart and allow you to feel Divine energy. That's the end goal of all these exercises. So, be creative. Be generous. Be the Divine spirit in a human body that you already are. Try it. I bet you'll like it!

♥ *Everyone values validation.*

Today I will talk to someone I don't know.

This exercise is to get you comfortable recognizing that we are all in this together. We all have needs, wants, desires, hopes, dreams, and experiences. We can help each other on this journey. We don't have to all be the same, to think the same, and like the same things. Diversity is so interesting! See what fascinating thing you can learn today. And, you may be surprised by what someone will find fascinating about you!

♥ *We are all in this together.*

Today I will volunteer 15 minutes of my time to assist someone.

Typically, when we think of volunteering to assist someone, we see them as being in need of assistance. It can bring up the feeling of being better than another person, even though that may be subconscious and unknown to you at the time. What you might desire is to see assisting someone as a collaboration or a cooperative effort. It's a desire to have everyone succeed and flourish. When you can see volunteering from this perspective, it brings forth a beautiful resonance of energy whereby the person you are assisting benefits simply from being in your presence. And, you benefit from theirs.

♥ *Volunteering is a collaboration or cooperative effort. You are helping and you are being helped.*

Today I will share.

Sharing is giving of you. For this expansion, you can share any way you like. You can share a story. You can share a recipe. You can share your time. You can share your experience. You can share your expertise. This is another way to help you remember that you matter. You have value, and you have a lot to offer. And, others do too. Together we rock!

♥ *You matter. You have value. What will you share of you?*

Today I will think of something most people don't know about me and I'll share it with someone.

People want to feel connected. You bond through experiences, shared beliefs and feelings, and through opening up and allowing someone to see who you really are and not just the façade you present to the world. By sharing something that is not commonly known about you with someone, you will most likely make them feel special and valued. That elicits connection. After sharing your story, invite the other person to share something about themselves.

♥ Are you willing to take down the façade of you and allow the authentic you to shine?

For example, I am named for Linda Darnell. She was an actress of a time. So now you know something about me most people - until now - didn't know about me. Doesn't that help you form your understanding of me? You draw conclusions about me from that and any tangent you can attach to it. It makes you feel like you know me better and that helps establish bonds of friendship and trust. Now it's your turn.

Today I will do something for the first time.

Doing something for the first time is very important to keep you engaged with life, consciously and with presence. It stimulates new neural pathways. And, it reminds you that life is about the adventure. There is so much to explore and experience. When you do something for the first time, you are (on some level of you) transported to that energy of wonder and awe that you had as a kid as you explored the world around you. That open and receptive and non-jaded state opens the flow of your energy to the most expanded version of you. It helps you connect to your choice point or that place beyond time and space where you chose how this life would play out for you (per Choice Point Creation Arts as discussed in the Chapter "How to Use This Book"). I imagine there are still a few things left that you could do for the first time!

♥ *Life is about the adventure.*

Today I will challenge myself.

We are creatures of habit. That's right! We are! We tend to do things the same way over and over - even as we change - because it's known and easy. To challenge ourselves seems like work.

I'd offer, however, that you can reconnect to when you knew challenging yourself was FUN. Kids enjoy a challenge. It's new. It's exciting. Something unexpected and great might come from it. And, even if it doesn't, kids intuitively know that it's still ok and that there is learning in everything (even if they can't yet express that verbally).

♥ *Let's reconnect to challenges being fun and exciting.*

So today, how would you like to challenge yourself? You don't have to climb Everest today! Just choose something a bit out of your comfort zone. Perhaps it would be to walk a half-mile farther. Perhaps it's to attempt a new recipe that had given you pause. Perhaps it's learning a new skill. You don't have to share your challenge with anyone. There is no failure. It's about reconnecting to that space of enjoying the new and being creative in daily life. You can discover a lot of fun new things with a challenge. I know you can do it! So, go forth and conquer.

Today I will write down three things on my bucket list.

Many people simply do not know what they want. They have become so disconnected from who they really are and what they really love and what they really desire that they can't tell you what they would create if they believed they could. Is that you?

To consciously create your life and circumstances – which is what I'm offering to help you with – you have to know what you want. Take some time today to think about that. Leave off the limits – it's too much money, I don't have the time, I no longer look good in a bathing suit, my work will suffer, etc. etc. etc. Go with what comes to you first. Write it down. There is something positive about writing things down. It helps you focus your thoughts and, on some level, shows you accountability. It's only three things.

Go!

♥ *What do you desire? No limits!*

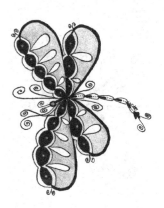

Today I will take a step towards my identified dream.

If you don't know what you desire, you will continually be waiting for something great to show up and be disappointed when it isn't just right. What do you want? That's often the most challenging thing for folks to pin down. Consequently, those same people often allow others to mold and guide their dreams.

♥ Energy likes action.

What do YOU want in life? Write it (them) down. Now do one thing that will get you a bit closer to having it in your life. For example, if you'd like to visit Bali, get a book on what to do in Bali or research it online. If you want to open a business, do something that would make that more likely to happen. Perhaps it would be to make an appointment with someone who has a successful business like the one you want and would be willing to share insight with you. It doesn't matter what it is. Energy likes action and forward movement. Establish a forward momentum toward your dream. Your energy will adjust to that in multiple ways and you will feel the empowerment. You are a creator. Create your dream – and one step at a time is perfectly fine!

Today I will be honest.

The Merriam-Webster dictionary defines honest as, "free from fraud and deception, genuine, real, marked by integrity, sincere". Does this describe you in all areas of your life? I believe most people would say no.

There is a difference between sharing everything and honesty. There are times when not sharing the entire truth is best for the other person (in your opinion). You can be honest and not share everything with everyone. People get confused about that. It is the underlying feeling you have about you as you make choices, both just for yourself and as they relate to others, that is important. If you feel that you are being authentic to you and your values and what you believe, that is honest even if you don't share the information. However, if you feel deceptive, then whether you are or not, the result internally will be the same. Energetically, it is not for your best.

♥ *To really open spiritually and intuitively, being authentic is important. Being authentic is being true to you. It's that simple.*

As you go through your day today, become aware of how you feel as you make choices and as you share information. Do you feel good about yourself, or do you have a twinge that says you are being deceptive? It can be a little tricky. But, if your intention is to act in the best interest of all concerned and you feel you have done that, then you're good energetically. It's when you feel that you are going against what you know is right that it can cascade energetically and really lower your vibration.

If you find that you are regularly feeling a bit off with what you are choosing, take a few quiet moments and ask

yourself where it is within you that you feel you are not being authentic (being who you know yourself to really be behind the façade you present to others). That's an important insight. Because, to really open spiritually and intuitively, being authentic is important and will serve you well. The more you are authentic, the more situations where you might be inclined to choose otherwise will just no longer be a part of your experiences. Remember the "like attracting like" concept of creating and manifesting? That's why you want to choose love and joy and peace. Because that is what you desire under the 3D representations of that. It's the same thing with honesty. Be honest and you attract honesty both in your experiences and in the people who are drawn to you and into your life. It matters.

♥ *Where are you comparing yourself to others and judging yourself against what you believe they offer and represent? If you are doing that, just know that all may not be as it seems. Many people have different personas given what situation they are in. Many people wear a mask that represents what they want you to believe. That would mean that you are comparing yourself to something that is not authentic. Just FYI…*

Today I will choose a virtue from the list below and exhibit it from my actions.

Though we aren't typically taught about virtues per se, we learn about virtues from early childhood. A virtue is defined as a quality that is considered morally good and/or desirable in a person. They come from ancestral teachings, faith teachings, family, cultural values and mores, societal expectations, etc. Lumped together, you might consider them a roadmap to becoming a "good person".

The thing is, virtues tend to become ingrained within our patterns of behavior and thinking, without conscious assistance. We make choices from an early age that are automatically categorized and cataloged by our brains in association with virtues. Given how we interpret our environment and experiences, sometimes those associations are skewed. That's when issues resulting from internal conflict can arise.

♥ *What do you consider to be your best three virtues? Are they part of your everyday life?*

One way to know what you believe about virtues is to get or make a list of virtues and see how you feel about each one. If you have any twinge of misgivings about one, look into that. Why do you feel the way you do about it? When did you develop the feelings? What was happening in your life at that time? Generally, most people agree that common virtues are desirable. If you don't agree, check into why. As long as your feelings are authentic to who you know yourself to be, you should be good to go. However, if you recognize a virtue is worthwhile, but you know you don't adhere to its quality, dig deep (see Chapter on Changing Beliefs and "Asking") to find out why that is. You may want to shift that. It's always your choice. But, knowledge and information upon which to base your choices are always helpful.

If you search for a list of virtues, you will find many. I have chosen just a few to list here that tie in beautifully to the purpose of these exercises. Choose one of these or search and find one of your own.

Authenticity

Awe

Compassion

Courage

Creativity

Encouragement

Gentleness

Graciousness

Honesty

Integrity

Joyfulness

Loyalty

Love

Peace

Respect

Thankfulness

Trust

Understanding

Unity

Vision

Wisdom

Wonder

♥

Wonder...

Awe...

Reconnecting to...

♥

That should give you plenty to choose from. If you want to get fancy, choose one you desire but don't feel is one of your stellar performers and practice that one. If you really want to see what you're made of, choose one you know you don't have and give it a go. My "go-to" virtues – and I didn't really think of them that way until writing this – are love and joy and peace – which you will see reflected in this book throughout. What are yours?

♥
Love...
Joy...
Peace...
♥

Today is a no negative judgment day!

It is truly amazing how often we judge – things, people, situations, ourselves – everything. So, today, be very aware of your thoughts. When you realize you are negatively judging something, say "No! I choose love" and intend that the change has been made. This is a way to both become aware of how much you judge, and also to become aware of what you are thinking in any given moment. That, then, will assist you in keeping your thoughts positive and uplifting and of a high vibration, which will help you to attract positive and joyful things into your life. Today see everything and everyone through rose-colored glasses!

♥ *Rose-colored glasses rock! Just saying… Mine come with sparkles…*

Today I will think of three statements to say to myself every day when I wake up for at least a month.

Your intention is powerful – probably much more powerful than you have ever imagined. When you decide to have a great day at the beginning of the day, and you intend for it to happen, the Universe is put on notice that you have made a choice for how you want life to show up for you. Energetically, you are setting the stage for success. When you regularly have the same desire, you begin to feel what it would feel like to have it actually happen more and more. As you do that, you are "feeding" the intention so it can grow and actualize.

Examples of the statements might be:

1. Today I will remember that everyone is doing the best they can with where they are physically, mentally, emotionally, and spiritually.
2. Today I will notice the small things that other people do that are helpful and nice.
3. Today, I will thank the Divine Energy of Creation when I notice things that I like.

or...

1. Today will be a great day.
2. Today I will be happy.
3. Today I will share my happiness with others.

The caveat here is to not get discouraged. Don't "fake it 'till you make it". If you're beginning to wonder if it will ever work, tap into the feeling of what it will be like when it *does* show up and be excited about it. Otherwise, you are throwing less than positive energy (i.e. lower vibrational energy) into the stew.

♥ *Your intention is powerful. Did you know you can energetically set the stage for your day with intention? Talk about conscious creation! Yea!*

Your result may be bitter and not savory like you intended. Give your stew the best possible opportunity to be stellar by adding fresh wholesome ingredients, just the right amount of spice, and be joyfully excited about what you have created being ready.

And, of course, tomorrow begin your day before you get out of bed by repeating the statements and know that your intention has begun to cook. Happy creating.

♥ What are you cooking today? Are you smelling it in anticipation? Are you seeing it beautifully presented? Can you almost taste it already? Are you excited for it to be ready? *That's the way to do it! Create away! You can do this! I know you can!*

Today I will notice every time I say, "I am _____".

Words are powerful. Very powerful. We associate meaning to words. We associate feelings to meaning. Then, you are left with the resulting beliefs with the fuel (feelings) to create.

What does all that mean for you right now? It means that *your words are powerful creative elements*. Your amazing brain takes your words, plugs in the known meaning and feelings, and develops beliefs about things given the experiences you are having. It does this with spoken words and your thoughts. Those beliefs are the building blocks for how you view your world and whether you see yourself as a victim of life and circumstances, or a person who summons what you desire through consciously directing your thoughts and feelings, knowing that thought and feeling derived from love and joy and peace will bring you experiences of like vibration.

Given all that, can you see how when you say "I am tired", you are sending out an energetic telegram to the Universe saying I want more tired? *How are you defining yourself?*

Try a little experiment. Say "I am love. I am joy. I am peace. I am beautiful. I am creative. I am amazing." How is your body feeling? Now if you change that and say "I am nothing. I am unworthy. I am hopeless. I am ugly. I am fat. I am undesirable." Not so good anymore, is it? The energy shifts instantly. (Here, I'd go back and repeat the first group! Maybe several times!) When you also add in the feelings of those words, they become exponentially more powerful. Really.

♥ *Your words are powerful creative elements. Add feeling to them and you have the rocket ready to lift off for your creation. The words "I am" are very defining and powerful. Make sure when you identify yourself with these words that you want what you are creating!*

♥ *I am love. I am joy. I am peace. I am beautiful. I am creative. I am amazing. I AM.*

So, it is important to recognize when you are sabotaging yourself. Your energy doesn't really take into account whether you know you are doing it or not. You don't have to be the "thought police". Once you become aware of what you are doing and practice choosing happier options, you will soon notice that you are doing it less and less. You are training your brain and ego that you desire positive thoughts and feelings – even if the attending situation doesn't seem to fit them. In that case, what can you find that is good in the situation?

For example, you have a fender bender. Instead of focusing on the repair needed and all the other things that you will need to do, focus on the fact that you didn't have a more involved wreck. Focus on the fact that no one was seriously hurt. You get the idea. It's not ignoring what is. It is choosing how you will react, and it is choosing the best of the situation as your focus – even as you handle whatever is needed. That may sound daunting. That's why it's important to practice. Notice, and then consciously choose the positive. Soon it will come naturally and you'll be helping your family and friends do it too. The other added bonus is that you will be putting in your "custom order" to the Universe for things that make your vibration higher and things that make you happy. That's a good deal!

♥ *What are you ordering today from the Universe?*

Today I will be and feel happy.

Take a moment today to be happy. No matter what your situation is or how you are feeling about things, pause. Take a deep breath and remember what it feels like to be happy. Let that feeling fill you completely. Then, choose to be grateful that you know what happiness feels like and choose to allow it to be in your day today. Then choose to take many moments!

Happiness matters. YOU matter. What you feel matters. Choose to have a happy moment and really feel it at that moment. Then, remember that you have choices. You can choose to allow yourself to be within the vibration of happiness, even as you take care of everyday matters. The more you resonate with and are in the vibration of joy and happiness, the more you attract the same.

Have a wonderful day filled with love, joy, happiness, and gratitude...

♥ *Happiness matters. Happiness is a great playmate with joy and kindness and compassion.*

Time to let you be you!

Beginning To Believe Expansion

The Beginning to Believe Expansion is designed to begin to take down the barriers to authenticity and living as who you really are.

♥ *We are living art.*

Today I will touch my hand. I will feel the life within.

Many of us believe that touching ourselves is a sin. So, we don't. Yet, we inhabit such amazing bodies. *We are works of art. We are living art. And, that art is alive and thriving.* When you touch your hand, do you feel that touch simultaneously anywhere else? How does it make you feel to do that? Is it uncomfortable, or does it bring up a sense of relief – finally there is permission?

Your body is your lifeline in this world. It allows you to experience and move through life – literally. It is amazing. And, it should be honored as such. Yet, all too often we criticize it. All too often we are shamed by it. All too often we take it for granted.

What if you and your body were a team? What if you and your body worked together to experience life to its full potential?

Wouldn't that be nice? Maybe you're already in that space. If so, congratulations! This exercise is still important for you from a spiritual perspective. Go the next step. Can you feel the life within? Can you feel your soul energy flowing through your body? Do you recognize your soul?

Today will help the brain disconnect from past non-serving beliefs about the body and your relationship to it.

♥ *You are not your body, but your body is your partner, whether you consciously realize it or not. The cells in your body are alive. Know that your actions and thoughts and feelings impact that life. Be conscious. Be respectful. Be aware. Be in love with your partner! The rewards will be evident.*

Today I will look in the mirror. Today I will see me.

This is a common exercise that therapists use to help people gauge their self-esteem and self-love. This can be a very challenging exercise for some. For some, the look in the mirror shows a stranger. They have become so disassociated with their own feelings and desires that they no longer recognize themselves.

How do you feel when you look in the mirror? Do you sway and go "Aaaa! Yea baby!" or do you recoil? Or are you numb? Really feel into the exercise. What do you feel? Where do you feel it? Does it hit you in the gut? Do you feel physically sick? Or does it bring up sadness?

♥ Any action outside of love has a core of fear. You are not your actions. But, you are responsible for them.

No matter the results, know that as you continue this journey with me, feelings of things other than love and joy and peace and contentment will dissipate. But, you have to take that first step and identify where you are with you. You are amazing. You are incredible. If you don't recognize that within yourself yet, I'd like to help you get there. I know you're great. And, yes, that inner voice may speak up now and say that you've done some things you weren't proud of. However, I would offer that in any given moment, you did the best you could with where you were physically, mentally, emotionally, and spiritually. Does that mean your actions get a pass? Not necessarily. It does mean, though, that you are not your actions.

Any action outside of love has a core of fear. What is the fear? Fear of not being enough? Fear of not being worthy? Fear of judgment? Fear of being alone? What is the fear? When you

can identify the fear, you can choose to release and resolve it. You can choose a path of love and kindness and compassion. People learn. People build on their experiences. You can too. Allow yourself the grace of compassion – even if you feel you don't deserve it. *You are a Divine Being having a human experience.* Be willing to own that. Your soul is so expanded. It is part of the Divine Energy of Creation – the energy of all life combined. You are that. Own that and *believe in your own worth – no matter what.* For so it is if you allow it to be…

♥ *Believe in your own worth – no matter what. I believe in your worth. Give yourself the ability to succeed and thrive. Consciously choose what YOU believe about you. How others define you is not the concern. How you define you is. Mistakes are mistakes. Not so loving choices are just that. Begin with your connection to the Divine Energy of Creation. You are part of that and so is everything else. And that is just Divine!*

Today I will look in the mirror and commit to being my own best friend.

I know. I know. You probably already have a best friend. Let me offer you a perspective you may not have thought of yet.

Friends are great. They each have different strengths. They each have specialized likes and dislikes. All that makes for great interest and support.

Yet, there are some aspects that are less optimal, such as the degree of loyalty and honesty, availability, and non-endearing personality quirks. But, because friendship is so valuable, most of us learn to take each friend with whatever they bring and whatever they are willing to offer.

All that said, what if there was a friend who was absolutely perfect for you in every way? What if this friend would always be there for you under any circumstances, loved everything you love, was good to go for anything you wanted when you wanted, was supremely loyal, and always had your back? Sounds awesome, right? You can have such a friend. And, in case you haven't guessed, it's you!

We don't typically think of being our own best friend. Yet, it makes perfect sense. Who knows you best? Who loves you most? Who values everything about you?

But wait... do you love yourself? Do you value you and what you have to offer? Do you enjoy your own company?

♥ Make sure your relationships are based on a foundation of self-love, self-honor, and self-respect. You deserve that. You are worthy of that. And, you should expect that of yourself.

♥ As a creator, it is your right to choose. Does that evoke feelings of obligation to choose well? If so, choose to release and resolve that and intend for all your choices to be from and for love and only that.

Perhaps the truth hurts. Perhaps you, because you think you know the real you, don't feel you deserve to be unconditionally loved. Perhaps you don't feel you have anything of real value to offer. Perhaps you feel that what you can project for others to see is more real to you than what you believe about yourself.

♥ How can you be an authentic friend and really allow others to know the "real" you if you don't love yourself and love what makes you uniquely you?

♥ "Today you are You, that is truer than true. There is no one alive who is Youer than You." Dr. Seuss

So, start there. Take a good look at what you believe about you. Would you choose you as a friend? If not, why? What is it you think isn't good enough? Be really honest. This is about changing your entire life for the better.

If you are not your own best friend first, how can you expect to even know how to be a great friend to someone else? How can you be an authentic friend and really allow others to know the "real" you if you don't love yourself and love what makes you uniquely you? This is really important.

We aren't taught to be our own best friend. Yet, some of us learn how to be because of our external experiences. The caveat with this is that you may come to feel that the *only* one who can be completely trusted is you. So, you make friends, but they are compartmentalized. Different people may know different parts of you. Or not. This is one way that you may consider yourself a friend to you.

However, a more healthy and expansive way is to really evaluate how you feel about you and how you feel about your relationships with others. Learn to love yourself unconditionally. From that love, trust yourself. From that love, enjoy yourself. From that love, know that you are worthy and deserving of the best life has to offer. Then, find friends who support that within you.

Instead of walling off most of your heart to protect it, and as a gesture of self-friendship, take the next step and really look at the core of why you feel that is the best way to live and relate (in self-protection mode). Then be a really good friend to yourself and heal the core that would keep you from being anything but open and honest and loving and compassionate. Does this mean sharing every detail of your life with everyone else? No. It means practicing proper discernment with others, but being completely honest with yourself.

You are amazing. *You have a uniqueness that allows anything you offer to be special.* When you know that about you, honor and love that about you, you become your own best friend. From that understanding and truth, you can then share you with others. And, you can share on your own terms, but from the space and vibration of authenticity and honoring the truth of you.

Love is a great equalizer. Make sure your relationships are on level playing fields. Make sure they are based on a foundation of self-love, self-honor, and self-respect. That has the potential to allow everyone to be a best friend in some capacity. How wonderful would it be to know that and feel that in all relationships? The choice is yours to make. Choose you. Why? Because you rock!

♥ *You are amazing. You have a uniqueness that allows anything you offer to be special. When you know that about you, honor and love that about you, you become your own best friend.*

♥ *Would you like to permanently shift into love and joy and peace? Wonder and awe are great friends with them.*

Today I will allow only positive thoughts.

It is amazing how many stray thoughts people have during a day. Can you relate? Those thoughts are helping to create your future. Your brain is not distinguishing between a conscious deliberate thought and a stray thought. And, it attaches feelings to those thoughts. *Thought plus feeling equals the magic formula for creating.* Consequently, it is important to become aware of your thoughts – all of them.

♥ What are you feeding your fears? You may need a new menu!

Part of the goal is to be able to distinguish between your intentional thoughts and rogue thoughts that just pop in. As you begin your spiritual journey and begin to tap into your spiritual gifts such as intuition, you will want to know "who's talking". Being able to recognize you is a key part of that.

You have an ego. We all do. And the ego's job is to protect you. As it does its job, it sometimes feels the need to instill fear and doubt to keep you from doing something out of the ordinary where the ego is unsure of how to keep you safe. As you begin to become aware of all the thoughts floating around in your head, you can also become aware of what you are consciously choosing to think, what the ego is suggesting, and other random thoughts. When you can easily distinguish thought origin, you can easily change what you do not want.

So today, every time you have a thought that is less than positive, say "No. I choose love (or joy or peace or kindness or compassion or etc.)". Make what you choose short and sweet. You won't always have a lot of time to choose something positive that is more specific. *Less than positive thoughts generate less than optimal feelings within the body.* Notice that. And, notice what happens within your body when you change a thought to a positive. You are both teaching and rewiring your brain to understand that you are choosing to feel good and you are choosing to be kind and compassionate and loving and joyful. Your body has cellular memory. It will remember the association between a positive thought and the feelings it generates, and it will distinguish that from those that are less positive and those associated feelings. With a bit of practice, your brain will alert you when you are having a less than positive thought and, eventually, it will auto-correct. Then you will shift into just not going that direction with thought at all. So, don't worry. I'm not having you train to be the thought police! We're just learning yet another way to shift permanently into love and joy and peace.

♥ *Thought plus feeling equals the magic formula for creating.*

Today I will say only positive things.

Speaking thoughts gives them a good dose of energetic power. Is what you are saying in line with what you want to create? If the thoughts aren't positive, I doubt it. So today, say only positive things.

♥ Speaking thoughts gives them a good dose of energetic power. Is what you are saying in line with what you want to create?

As you go through your day, see if you notice an upswing in the energy of your day. Are more things going your way than usual? Do people seem nicer today? Does that parking space just magically appear? How about the "cradle" in traffic where there is heavy traffic in front and behind you but not around you? Notice what goes on and whether it is more positive than usual.

When your focus is on the positive, your thinking and vocalization reflect that. As you consciously choose the positive and uplifting, you are choosing to experience life from a higher vibration. Since like attracts like in this energetic context, guess what? You are creating a future with more positive experiences. Woohoo! You go! Not as hard as you thought is it?

♥ Everything is energy.

Today I will smile more often than yesterday, and I will feel the internal joyful change within me each time.

Your brain recognizes patterns. Babies smile when they are happy. They do that from the start. So, *your brain is hardwired to recognize a smile as a representation of a potentially happy moment.* It literally releases hormones and neurotransmitters that facilitate and support happy feelings. That said, if you smile more, your body will respond in kind. And, as you consciously repeat an action, the brain begins to register the action as a pattern and as something you desire. It begins to notice what brings on these occurrences and begins to record this information. Your brain then helps you to notice times when these "happiness actions" occur. With that conscious acknowledgement of the cause of happiness, your vibration rises. And, as that happens, you begin to create and manifest more of the same in your life. Smiling has a lot of positive physiological, emotional, mental, and spiritual responses. That also goes for people who see others smile, and especially those for whom a smile is specific. So, smile. You'll like it and so will everyone else. And... added bonus...you are even more beautiful when you smile! Win-win!

♥ *When you smile, your beauty shines from without and within.*

Today I will look around my home and, in my closets, to identify things I love and those I do not. If I find things I do not love, I will consciously choose whether to continue to keep them. If I decide to keep them, I will identify why I am making this choice.

We tend to be creatures of habit. We tend to take what seems to be the easy route. There is nothing bad or wrong about that. However, energetically, that may work against us.

♥ *What do you have in your home that opens your heart and sings the song of you?*

As I have been saying, everything is energy. Inanimate objects are energy and they hold energy as well. When you look at an item such as a picture, and you love it, your heart opens and you radiate out the energy of love to everything around you – automatically. Yet, when you look at a picture you do not love you do the same, just in reverse. As you do either, you change the collective energy and vibration of your living space. As you can guess or as you already know, living in energies of a higher frequency support health, balance, harmony, kindness, joy, peacefulness, and love (among other wonderful things). You can feel it. Your pets can feel it. Visitors to your home can feel it.

Another thing to consider is that you change over time. What you once loved might not resonate any longer. But, if you sold or donated or gave it to someone else, they might absolutely love it. And, their hearts would send you love. It's true, whether done consciously or not. That also allows you space for bringing in something new that you do now truly love. Then, every time you look at it, your heart opens and sings the song of you. How awesome is that?

So, what's your choice?

♥ *Home is where you relax into Being and rejuvenate.*

Today I will bless my food and drink before tasting.

You are 90% water. Did you know that? And, the food you eat is the fuel you offer to your beautiful body machine. Don't you want to offer it the best for optimal efficiency and functioning?

I know for some of you those fries and pizza are calling you and just won't pipe down! But, there are other things you can do to support your body. One is to bless your food and drink.

♥ Blessing your food and drink is an expression of love – gratitude for the gift, and self-love. It's a win-win.

Imagine for a moment what it took, from the very beginning, to get any drink or any food to you. Consider all the people involved. Consider the farmers. Consider those who make the laws that govern the roads. Consider those who voted for them. Consider the truck drivers. Consider those who make the containers. Consider the trees and other natural materials used to make those containers. Consider the rain. Consider the way rain is absorbed into and even stored underground. Consider the clouds. Consider everything! *When you truly look at it, everybody and everything is in some way responsible and played a part in you getting the food and drink you are about to enjoy.* Truly!

So now consider the energy of all those people and everything else. Consider the differences in resonance. As your food and drink make their way to you, they absorb energies. That is what you take in. That's where blessing your food and drink beforehand comes in.

When you bless your food, ask to go back to "before the beginning" (of everything or to your "choice point") and see the blessing and clearing as a beautiful white light that flows from that point of origin into the now, clearing the energies absorbed as what you are about to take in makes its way from the ground into the mother plant, and then as it is harvested, and then as it is processed, and then as it is sold, and then as it travels, and then as you purchase it, and then as you store it until time to eat. Bless it with beautiful white light from the Divine Energy of Creation. Imagine it filled and glowing with this light and imagine that light then filling your body as you enjoy your food. Imagine the same for water as it cycles through its life and finds its way into your home. Beautiful cleansing and nourishing white light. Imagine it restoring lost nutrients, and the food and drink being brought back to their original Divine blueprint.

♥ *Your food and drink are energy and they absorb energy. Wouldn't it be nice to know that they are offering you what was originally intended in their Divine blueprint?*

Today I will take a shower and visualize the water washing away my cares.

This exercise is a favorite of mine. I love the feel of water. I also love that I can visualize any cares, any burdens, any issues being literally washed away. It is your "Calgon take me away" * moment in the shower. The visualization can actually clear your energy which will also make you feel better. And, you'll be clean when you're through!

For any reader who may be worried about the earth and dousing it with negative energy, don't worry. Nature is a wonderful natural purifier. Just give thanks to the earth for offering you that gift. No need to be concerned.

*From a commercial long ago where a lady has had it with all the distress of the day. She says "Calgon take me away." You next see her in a bathtub with bubbles and she can finally relax because she is using Calgon in the bath water. Now you know!

♥ *Water is life. Water offers life. And water sustains life. In addition, water is fabulously beautiful when clear, harmonized and balanced (think of snowflakes). Your energy impacts water and the energy of water can impact you. Water is an AMAZING partner. (check out the work of Dr. Masaru Emoto)*

Today I will open a book and see what message it brings to me.

This is one of my favorite ways to get you started "hearing" messages from the Divine Energy of Creation and your own Divine nature (as well as Spirit in its many forms).

When you would like to know the direction in which your soul wants you to go or you would like a general message from your soul (or an angel or guide, etc.), set an intention that you will open the book to a page that will offer that insight or message and you will be drawn to the location on the page that is most appropriate. Hold the book and imagine your heart reaching out and touching the book, and then open to any page as you are guided. Until you are able to receive messages in other ways, this is a great jumping off point. It worked beautifully for me and seemed to be perfect every time.

Spiritual and inspirational books are exceptionally good for this type of practice. It helps if it is a book of quotations (some of my favorites are listed in the back of this book). There are countless options, including this book after you finish it! Be sure to offer thanks for the message you receive.

Interestingly enough, I love books. I would find myself in the bookstore and I would feel drawn to a particular book. I'd purchase my treasure. But, often I'd get home and wouldn't take the time to read it. I know now I was receiving the energy embedded within the book from the message and energy of the author. However, there was yet another value.

♥ Be open to all possibilities.

♥ Be present. Be open. Be appreciative. Allow your soul to show you truth.

Occasionally, I would wake up in the middle of the night and have a question I really wanted answered. I wouldn't be able to sleep. I'd find myself before my bookcase and, once again, I'd be drawn to a particular book. Every time I would find my answer in the book! Typically, I'd then read the entire book and the message was perfect. So... allow Spirit to work through you to assist you. Pay attention! If you feel drawn to something, there is a reason. You'll soon learn what is then wanted from you on your end (ex. The exact book I needed, with the exact answer I needed, was on my bookshelf in the middle of the night! All I had to do was allow myself to be guided to it when the time was right.) I find all this fabulous! ...and oh so helpful!

If you pay attention to what you are feeling, all this will flow for you and it won't seem daunting and you won't be feeling "How am I supposed to figure that out!". Truly. Believe. Trust. Be willing to embrace your wisdom and power. And just let go and "let God". Desire that and feel it as if that were already in place for you. Then, watch it happen. It truly will if you allow it to be.

♥ *If you let them, the answers will come! It can actually be a fun game when you are learning. Don't take it so seriously. If you are so very serious, that's your order to the Universe. If you look at it as a delightful hide and seek game (but one you always win!), then your order coming up will be very different. Your life. Your choice. Choose fun! Win-win!*

Today I will ask the Divine Energy of Creation (God, Creator, Allah, the Universe, Source, etc.) what it wants me to know for today.

When I was in the early stages of my spiritual exploration, I would get comfortable propped up in bed, open a document program on my laptop, and ask the Divine Energy of Creation what beliefs I needed to work on that day. I would begin to write whatever came to me. I would expect to know what to write and I would patiently sit there until something came. If I was having a really challenging time with it, I'd say "I want to know beliefs about worthiness" (or trust, or what I believed about women or men, or what I believed to be true about me, etc.). As I did this more and more, it became easier and easier. It was incredibly insightful.

Even if you are not yet fully aligned with your soul energy where beliefs can automatically resolve, it is still incredibly important to begin to learn what you do and do not believe. As you discover your beliefs, you can start by desiring to change those beliefs you do not want and intend to have the ones you do want. Become proactive. And trust that you are the creator of your life experiences so you can choose what you do and do not want.

Eventually, you will begin to ask yourself about your beliefs related to anything that is happening in your life that is not working as you would like it to work. Once you know what a situation is presenting (i.e. what beliefs is it showing you), you can choose to change those beliefs and the associated

♥ If you are willing to embrace your wisdom and power, your soul will work with you hand-in-hand every day. Ask yourself if you are ready. If you think "yes" but don't then feel elated and excited, you might ask yourself what would happen if your soul was your partner and you were consciously aware of it. What is the fear?

♥ Sometimes what you want to know and what the Divine wants you to know are the same. And, sometimes they are not. Just know that your soul has your back even if you blame your soul for any distress you have experienced (this would probably be subconsciously). If you just can't seem to get excited about reconnecting consciously to your soul, ask if you blame your soul for abandoning you and not protecting you. Sometimes we even blame our soul for things we want not showing up for us, like great wealth. But, as you grow in understanding and truth, you will know it's not about your soul. It's about your beliefs and feelings.

feelings, and usually similar types of situations will no longer show up for you. Why? Because you took notice of what your beliefs related to the issue were (and what they wanted to point out to you) and you chose, with your intention, what you wanted and what you did not.

I know, if you're reading this now, you probably want some type of change in your life. Are you willing to take a chance on you? Give yourself some credit. You're smart. If you ask for guidance from your soul and the Divine Energy of Creation *and then listen*, you will get the answers you want. Don't limit the way the answers come to you either. Perhaps you hear a news story that resonates. Perhaps someone brings up the topic in conversation. There are so many ways that you are guided and assisted. Be open to all possibilities and become aware. Awareness is key. Desire. Ask. Listen. And then act.

Today I will meditate.

I have an expanded view of what meditation really is all about. I do not enjoy sitting quietly and breathing in and out with candles burning and soft music playing. I prefer other ways to meditate. I especially like going for a quiet walk in the woods by myself. I like to really hear the birds. I like to see ferns ready to unfurl. I like to see creatures I have never seen before. I like to notice the changes that happen day to day. To me, that is a meditative process. It is calming. My only thoughts go to appreciation and love for all that surrounds me. My heart is bursting with love. In that state, I know the Divine Energy of Creation. In that state, I know myself. And, I like what I know.

♥ *Be present. Be open. Be appreciative. Allow your soul to show you truth.*

What would do that for you? There are no rules. You know you better than anyone else. *Be present. Be open. Be appreciative. Allow your soul to show you truth.* You are a focus of your soul energy in the here and now. Allow yourself to flow your "here and now focus" to that more expanded version of yourself and allow your imagination to show you the connection between your soul and the energy of all life everywhere. You are they and they are you.

Today I will see life from the perspective of a plant.

Plants are such loving and giving and beautiful life forms. Think of what your life would be like without plants. They aren't just food. They provide wood, for instance, which is used for homes and furniture and to support fire. They help provide oxygen for us to breathe. They provide a variety of other services as well. When you really take the time to consider them, they are interwoven into just about everything.

♥ *Plants are interwoven into just about everything in some way. Hug a plant today!*

So today, think of not only their value and service but also how it would feel to be a plant. Think about how they are typically treated. How would it make you feel?

This is important because as you open to your spiritual gifts, an appreciation for all life is important. *We are all part of the gorgeous tapestry of life – all of us.* Think of what that tapestry would look like without plants. This will open your eyes to a new and more comprehensive view of life as you have come to know it. You may even find that the next time you see a plant, you thank it for its service!

Today I will see life from the perspective of an animal.

As with plants, so too with animals. We tend to think of animals as more like us than plants. But, it's all perspective. Animals have been important to humans since the beginning of time. Think of the accomplishments made by partnering with animals. Think of the various types of service they provide. They deserve respect and to be seen as valuable to life. What would it feel like to be an animal? What would life look like from the perspective of an animal? Choose one. It may be an eye-opening experience.

As you think of animals, don't forget insects. Think of all the plants that depend on them. And, as you have come to understand, plants are necessary for our survival.

The cycles of nature coordinate and include plants, animals, and insects and other life forms. We are not able to survive independently, even though we may think so. To develop a respect for that is to begin to see life from a more spiritual perspective. It will help you to live in a state of respectful gratitude. And, hopefully, you have already come to know, through the exercises presented in this book, that gratitude will get you everything!

Note: This exercise is similar to the exercise in the "First Expansion" series where you did something nice for an animal. You might choose to re-read that exercise in conjunction with this exercise.

♥ *All things are part of all things.*

♥ *Does a four-legged angel live with you? If yes, give thanks for that special blessing! If not, there are many waiting for that special forever home in the shelters. Such unconditional love they bring and share and generate… You have so much love to share!*

Today I will feel the elements.

So today may be a stretch at first. I'm not suggesting that you go stand in the rain or play in the dirt or bask in the sun or open your windows. What I am suggesting is that, whatever weather shows up for you today in your area of the world, imagine feeling it. Imagine feeling what *it* feels like.

♥ The Divine sun is always shining for you. The Divine earth always holds you steady. The Divine rain always washes you into grace. The Divine wind always has your back.

Imagine that you are the rain. Imagine what it would feel like. Are you cold? As the rain do you even experience wetness? How does it feel to hit the earth? Is it a happy reunion? What happens then? How does it feel to go into the body as water?

What would it feel like to be air? How would it feel to be inhaled by so many? How would it feel to flow around trees and leaves and homes and cars?

What would it feel like to be the earth? Compacted together, you have the earth per se. What would that feel like? How would you feel about how people treat you? As dirt, what would that feel like? Imagine the ways dirt is used and moved and manipulated. How does that feel?

Fire. What would it feel like to be fire? Would you focus on destruction, or on providing a source of life-giving as people keep warm and cook food? Do you experience heat? What does it feel like when you can be turned on and off by others at will?

This exercise is designed to get you to begin noticing all the incredible gifts around you. And, to notice how you relate to them and if you even notice them, or if you take them for granted.

Part of becoming more attuned to your spiritual nature is to begin to understand that *all things are part of all things*. We all, even if it is in the most minute way, play a part in each other's lives. And, it is time to begin to appreciate the gifts of nature and how they impact your life every moment of every day.

♥ *What would it be like to be Nature (all of it together as a living thriving energy)?*

Today I will look at the weather, and the situations around me, and remember that I am not alone.

Remember when you first figured out that the sun was always shining even if it was cloudy or nighttime? If you experienced it as I did, you were amazed and thrilled. It was a hidden mystery brought to light. Well… you know where I'm going with this, right?

Even if you cannot see the hand of the Divine in what is happening to and around you, that love, that support, that peace, and that joy are still there. That energy hasn't abandoned you. That energy hasn't forgotten you. That energy hasn't deemed you unworthy or undeserving. *It's simply that you are out of alignment with it and the clouds of non-serving beliefs are obstructing your view.* That's all.

♥ *Don't let the clouds of non-serving beliefs obstruct your view.*

If you choose not to deal with the beliefs head on, at least do what makes you joyous (remember, happy is from without, so you want the deeper and more rich and whole emotion of joy, even though they often walk hand in hand) and do that as much as you possibly can. Even if you can't do a specific activity that generates that feeling and Being, at least think about it – not in an "I don't have" kind of way but in a "I love that" kind of way. Eventually that will raise your vibration and, hopefully, will get you to a level where nothing but that can exist, and the non-serving beliefs will automatically resolve. That's not always the most direct or expedient way, but it can work.

Some people feel that their past and even their present are just too painful to look at. You don't have to relive the experiences. But, acknowledging them brings them out of the deep recesses of your energy, where you have hidden them well, and allows them to say goodbye permanently, if you desire and allow it.

Why wouldn't you desire it? Because it is serving you in some way. Many times, it is so you won't forget the trauma and wounds so that you can hold onto the anger and somehow, someway, exact restitution – even in the hereafter. Is that really helping you now?

What if energy automatically re-balances? It may not be in the timeframe you desire – RIGHT NOW – but it will re-balance. Some call it karma. But, we've come to assign to karma the "eye for an eye, tooth for a tooth" energy. I would offer that there is no karma like that. There is, however, *equal and equitable energy re-balancing*. For us to apply hate and anger and fear and the like to it just ensures it will take longer to re-establish than it would otherwise. Ask for Divine love to fill the deep dark blank recesses of your hurt and pain and anger and hate and clear and re-balance that energy within you (note here: for you only; the rest will automatically take care of itself).

♥ *Did you know you have a spiritual team ready, willing, and able to assist you? All you need to do is ask for their help. They won't intrude, but they happily respond to your requests.*

So, remember, the Divine Energy of Creation – Creator, God, Allah, and by any other name – is ALWAYS present. Whether you can see or hear or feel or sense that presence is irrelevant. It is there/here and you are completely and absolutely loved and supported and embraced at all times. There is no ebb and flow to that. It just is. There is also a beloved contingent of "spiritual assistants" who, whether visible to you or not, assist you and are working to guide you and support you.

For today, set aside any thoughts or feelings of disbelief and trust that all this is true. And, for today, have this be your reality. Notice how you feel. Notice if things change for you for the better. Notice synchronicities. I have faith you will come to know that *the Divine sun is always shining for you and you can look past the clouds of life to access that energy anytime and anyplace.*

Then, if you choose, you can allow the weather to remind you every day of that unconditional and never-ending love that is always there for you. What a lovely partnership!

♥ *The Divine sun is always shining for you.*

Today I will see life from the perspective that every person is doing the best they can, in any given moment, given where they are physically, mentally, emotionally, and spiritually.

Let's state that again because it is critically important. Every person is doing the best they can, in any given moment, given where they are physically, mentally, emotionally, and spiritually. The actions of a person don't define them; they just show you where the fear is (resides).

So, when you see people from this perspective, you can see beyond their actions. You can do whatever you feel you need to do related to their actions to make you continue to feel authentic and in line with your values. But, you can also see that the person is worthy – worthy of love, worthy of compassion, worthy of peace. This view allows you to live in peace, no matter the circumstances. As you respond to injustice and imbalance and intolerable circumstances from this space, you are able to take action within compassion and hold your own values intact. It is as the sages of old reacted – though their actions may not have been as they would be today. The outward social and cultural environments change and evolve over time and set the flavor of respectability.

Feeling road rage? How could you possibly know, in that moment, the root cause of that angst and willingness to self-inflict pain through attempting to release rage and anger and disillusionment and despair by the perception of self-generated false power? You can't. So instead of judging, do what you feel

♥ *Everyone is a Divine Being having a human experience. From the 3D view, you probably do not know all the factors going into the behaviors of others. Have compassion for you and learn to see others from the perspective of the soul. You deserve that.*

you need to do to address the issue and protect yourself and visualize that person/consciousness as a person worthy of love and receiving it from the Divine in that moment, or as the situation unfolds. You are capable of responding to the situation and offering love (as part of the Divine) simultaneously. You are capable of seeing injustice and imbalance and understanding the more expanded truth of it simultaneously. And, as you recognize this within yourself and begin to embrace it as truth, your experiences will change because you will have exposed the core of what each experience was there to show.

Still not sure? Think about a time when you acted inappropriately. Was it only about the situation at hand or was it built on underlying fears, insecurities, past occurrences, or other factors? If you are truly honest with yourself, there is always more. Everything is not as clear-cut as it may seem. But, as you open to these truths, you also open to a more expanded view of what is happening. That fosters and nurtures compassion, both for others and for yourself. That fosters and nurtures a more expanded view of love and what love really is versus what you think it is.

You don't need to be a doormat or victim. But as situations present for you to choose those options, remember that you have infinite choices. Train yourself to see life in this way. It will serve you well and bring you much needed and desired peace – both inner and outer. It is how the Universe works per Universal Law.

Believe. Trust. Feel. Embrace. Act. Live authentically, purposefully, and with great joy and self-love. You deserve it and are worthy of it all.

♥ *It's not selfish to love you. In fact, it's generous. You can only offer the best of you if you know who you are, and you love who you are.*

Today I will listen to people with the intention to really understand, hear, see and feel what they mean and what they want to share.

We have become so distracted. We have so much information coming at us from all directions that we subconsciously set up all kinds of filters to help us navigate the deluge. And so, our face-to-face conversations may suffer. We may be looking at someone and we hear what he or she says, and we can respond, but we don't really *feel* what is meant and what the person wanted to share. It's almost robotic. We can even repeat the conversation, but there is not the empathy that was desired from the sharing.

♥ *Honoring the journey of another is an act of love.*

When you can honor the journey of another and respect their choices, and when you show that by allowing them to connect with you in a state of empathy and kindness and compassion, you are giving them a gift that is so much more than just a conversation. You make them feel valued. Everyone needs that. Everyone wants to be acknowledged. It doesn't mean you have to dwell on their non-positive indulgences. It only means to really pay attention and allow them to feel that you care. You don't have to agree either. Just acknowledge. *Give them the gift of you.* This is a great beginning to learn what it feels like to open your heart to others.

♥ *You are not alone. Everyone is here for you. And, you are here for everyone. How amazing is that?*

Today I will forgive myself.

This is a really interesting one. We are taught about forgiveness at an early age. But, there is always a feeling of something "wrong" that needs to be "fixed". I would offer that forgiveness is a man-made concept to allow us to move forward in life when we feel wronged.

In actuality, there is nothing to forgive. *If you believe that we choose our experiences and the people with whom we have them, then forgiveness as we have come to know it is a non-issue.* Yet, that is a challenging construct for many.

♥ Choose to love yourself. Choose to understand from a more expanded perspective. Choose you.

We want to believe that if we forgive others, they will forgive us. And, we want to believe that if we forgive others, we get "God points" and that God will look favorably on us. In a way, that fits into the construct I have presented. If you "forgive" another, you take a path of kindness and compassion instead of hate and anger. That choice is of a higher vibration than one of hate and anger. That raises your vibration and that will attract people and energies into your experience that match or exceed that vibration.

Well, you say, if we already chose those people and experiences, how can it be that we will attract something that is potentially different as we raise our vibration? Free will. Yes, we made "contracts" and agreements with others to help us learn and grow and experience. What if, in the midst of those experiences, we decide that we are tired of learning through pain and suffering? What if we decide we want to experience and learn with grace and ease and fun and joy and wonderful abundance? We can choose that. Raising our vibration will assist.

So, that said, forgiveness as we know it has value. But, in a more expanded sense, there really is no forgiveness. There is no karmic restitution as we currently think of it. It is merely a balancing and harmonization of energies that have gotten way off track - from joy and peace and love.

Are there places during your life experience where you feel regret or disappointment in yourself, or guilt? If so, choose today to allow all that to rebalance. Choose to understand that you were doing the best you could with where you were physically, mentally, emotionally, and spiritually in each and every moment. And, know you can choose to release the regret, disappointment, and/or guilt just by the desire and the understanding of how you came to have the experience in the first place. Choose to love yourself. Choose to understand a more expanded perspective on life and life experiences. Choose to believe in you. Choose self-empowerment from this moment forward. For so it is if you choose and allow it to be…

♥ *Love you more…*

Today I will forgive someone else.

As you "forgave" yourself yesterday, use the same understanding and thinking to forgive someone else today. Remember and know in your heart that they were doing the best they could in that moment with where they were physically, mentally, emotionally, and spiritually.

♥ *I choose love. I choose joy. I choose peace.*

♥ *Forgiveness is self-love.*

Releasing yourself from the ties to hate and anger will benefit you in so many ways. You will be doing yourself a favor. And remember, forgiving someone doesn't mean you condone the action or situation. It simply means that you can see a more expanded version of why they might have chosen as they did, and you understand that you are not privy to all that went into that choice. This holds true even in the most seemingly unforgivable situations. It's not about what happened. It's about your understanding of how the energy of the Divine sees what happened. *It's about opening your heart to the understanding that any action that hurts another originates from fear on some level* and that impacts a person physically, emotionally, mentally, and spiritually. We have all experienced fear and we know what it feels like. Some fear is deeply buried or hidden within our subconscious and a person may no longer be aware it is even there. The origins of that fear (or those fears) may even be unrelated to the current action – from a logical perspective. So, know that it is not your place to judge. You never have to support the action. But, *teach yourself how to have compassion for those who have not yet dealt with their fears*. You won't have to then go to tea with them. But, you can treat yourself because you have loved you more and you are learning to live consciously as the spark of the Divine that you are.

Today I will be grateful for everything that comes my way.

Today's exercise seems to be easier than it may turn out to be. If you read it carefully, it says "everything" that comes my way. Being grateful for everything that comes your way – even if it is something you do not desire – will help you shift into a "state of gratitude". *A state of gratitude, to me, is a way of living. It is recognizing that everything that is in your purview was ultimately created by you, whether consciously or not.* It is being grateful when something you do not desire shows up, that the Universe is showing you where you are creating this type of situation.

♥ *Are you living in a state of respectful gratitude?*

If such a thing or occurrence shows up, look at how it makes you feel. What fear is it bringing to the surface (for in the end analysis, fear is always the core)? When did you first experience a fear like this? That is where you need to look to identify the cause of your creations that do not serve you. What were you doing? Who was involved? How did you feel? Why are you not allowing the fear to resolve? What purpose does it serve? If it is something physical, look at the part of the body involved. Is it a leg? Perhaps you are fearful of moving forward. Then look at why that would be. What would happen if you did move forward? This is the type process to use to uncover what is really governing your subconscious creations. *Use what shows up in your life to guide you to the starting point.* And, be grateful.

Eventually, you won't curse "bad" situations. You will simply go "I wonder what this is showing me…" and you will look to uncover the core fear. Then you will consciously choose to release and resolve the fear. You will have your intention be that all your energy will work with you to do just that, and you will consider it done and be grateful. That is living in a state of gratitude. Additionally, when you are consistently in that state, you significantly reduce your negative thoughts and feelings which raises your vibration and, thus, will attract a higher level of vibrational experience to you, and what you subconsciously create will be more joyful and loving and peaceful and compassionate and fun. Sounds like a fine plan to me!

Gratitude is one of the highest vibrations. *Joyful gratitude*, where you are so thankful and so happy about it, raises that level even more. Since your energy, your vibration and frequency, resonate with all other energies, there is a synergy between your energy and what is attracted to your energy. The higher your vibration, the more you attract higher energy vibrations. The opposite is also true.

♥ *Joyful gratitude! Woohoo! Love it, love it, love it!*

Today I will expect good things to unfold for me in every way.

You create your day from your thoughts and feelings. Your thoughts and feelings create and guide your energetic vibration and frequency and that determines what you attract to you. Everything you think and do and say and feel matters. You can breathe! It's all good. Hang in there with me. You've got this!

As you begin your spiritual journey, you may not consciously recognize what you are really thinking and feeling in every moment. But as you intend to notice what you are thinking and feeling, and you practice consciously choosing those thoughts and feelings in the moment, you will soon notice - with joyful gratitude - how you are creating all that you experience. From that realization, you will also understand that you are empowering yourself. You are choosing for you and you choose what makes you happy. You choose "good things" (at least I trust you do!).

*♥ Joyful gratitude rocks! What can you be joyful about and thankful for today? Is **everything** too much of a stretch? If so, stretch those joyful and gratitude muscles in every way you can!*

Expectation of good things in every moment is training your brain to look for the good in things. *As you look for the good, find the good, appreciate the good, and react to the good, you are sending out the energy to the Divine Energy of Creation that this is what you desire, and you want more.* You are setting in motion forces that will align all that is required to make your dreams come true. How wonderful! What a good thing!

Today I will think of something I want, and I will uncover whether or not I really want it.

Here is a really good exercise that will help you discover why what you want to create may not be showing up. Sometimes, on one hand we want something, but on the other hand we have a fear about it – one we may not even know about.

♥ Sometimes, we have a push-pull energy within us. Part of us wants one thing and part of us wants the opposite. The challenge is that these internal struggles can be fought within the subconscious. So, if something isn't working as you'd like, deep dive into why it may not be. What would your experience be like if it presented exactly as you envision?

For example, say you desire to be an artist. You may feel you have the skill set and the tools, yet you just can't seem to get a break with displaying your art and getting the recognition you feel you deserve. Look at what the fear might be. Are you fearful that you will be judged? Are you fearful that you will be judged unfairly? Are you fearful that your art expresses your most deep and personal and intimate feelings and that you will be vulnerable and not safe? Are you fearful that you just aren't good enough to compete? Are you fearful that you will be consumed with the expectations and desires of others and you will no longer be free to pursue your art as you enjoy? Those type fears can manifest as roadblocks to your dream. On the one hand you create gorgeous art, but on the other you are creating blocks that will keep you from the full expression of that due to fear.

Or, what if your dream is to visit the North Pole, but you don't like to travel. If you know you don't like to travel, and the visit isn't worth the travel, then take that dream off your list. It's better to have a list that you will create than to have the warring energies of wanting and not wanting simultaneously.

So, today choose something you think you want and dive into any fears that might be attached to it so you can decide if you *actually do* want it or you just like the thought of it. It's important for creating the life you desire.

♥ *I love me! I am worthy! I am generous! I am beautiful! I am amazing! I am a creator! I rock! Woohooscoobydoo!!!*

Today I will think of something specific I'd like to have happen and expect it all day.

This is getting into creating what you desire in the most simple way. Think of something simple with an actual likelihood of happening. It could be something like having your favorite song play on the radio or having someone ask if you'd like to go out to dinner or anything like that. The reason I say "with an actual likelihood of happening" is that as you have success with this technique, it begins to resolve your disbelief automatically. As that happens, you open to the possibility of it more and you think about it more. As you do that, guess what?! It not only happens more (because often times these things do happen in response to your thoughts, but you don't notice them, or you discount them) but you begin to consciously believe it is possible for you and your feelings deepen.

♥ When you expect good things, it's setting your day's foundation to support and attract and embrace energies that bring situations and conversations and experiences that will make you happy. I love that! Don't you?

Feelings? Yes. *Feelings are the fuel for the fire of creation.* A thought alone is not likely to do it. But, when you add expectations and what it would feel like in every way to have it happen to you in the timeframe given (i.e. today), you are activating your own powers of creation. Some call this manifesting. I call it creation because you are creating it via your desires, thoughts, and feelings. Then, it just hangs out until you connect with the joyous feelings of having it to fuel it into the here and now. When you connect to the vibration of joy (and that means really feeling it), you are accessing a part of the Divine Energy of Creation – the energy of all life combined, also known as Creator, God, Allah, and by any other name. That energy is all powerful. Only a teeny tiny droplet of that energy is more than enough to create anything you desire. I know. It's a stretch to overcome a lifetime of cultural, environmental, formal, religious, and familial teachings that tell you "that's crazy". But, what if it weren't? What about those who thought the world was flat? What if no one had challenged that assumption and set out to see if it actually was true? Just saying…

There are many techniques associated with creating what you want and then manifesting it. This is one of them. Typically, when we think of something we want, we are looking at it from the sense of not having it or lack of it. The energy of that is not helpful for creating it in your life now. What is helpful is to be in a state of gratitude that it is already on its way, in perfect Divine timing for your best experience. So, if you can't envision yourself enjoying it as if it had arrived, imagine that everything is lining up for it to come to you, and be excited and happy about that.

♥ Excited expectation infused with gratitude for the arrival of your desire will get the job done.

And, don't fall into a "time" trap. We want what we want, and we want it now. But remember, you are almost never the only one impacted with what you desire and how it shows up. Give the Universe a break. Be in excited expectation. If it takes a month, it takes a month. Your beliefs and feelings impact your ability and willingness to allow it to come into physical manifestation. It could be instantaneous or not. Don't judge. Don't react. Just intend to allow and accept with gratitude.

If you get really impatient, ask yourself how it serves you to not have what you want. What is the fear or undesired consequence? For example, if you chose to be able to heal others instantly, do you fear never having any private time? Do you fear having to turn away deserving people – including family and friends – so you can have a life? Are you afraid of the expectations of others? Would you fear for your safety? What may seem so simple may be far more complicated when you add in your beliefs and feelings and thought patterns. Go easy on yourself and the Universe.

The exercises in this book will guide you to success. Keep going and smile!

♥ *I think I can. I KNOW I can. EUREKA! I'VE DONE IT!*

Today I will think of something I believe to be impossible and imagine it coming true.

Now this is a tricky one because of your likely beliefs. The goal here is to expose you to the concept of there being no limits to what you can create (as long as it is conceived within love and from a space of love). Most people, I'd say, don't believe that. Plus, in order to overcome those ingrained mass consciousness beliefs, the person who would like to create what is considered impossible will have cleared a lot of personal limiting beliefs and feelings and would truly believe anything is possible (see the Chapter on Changing Beliefs and "Asking"). They will also have looked at what would happen if the impossible did happen. Ah. Yes. There it is. *If the impossible is possible, is anything you believe true?* Have you been living a lie? So, if you keep the impossible as impossible, your world as you know it can remain intact and not explode. Right?

The easiest example to offer is that of the story of Jesus walking on water. Do you believe that happened or do you believe it is a parable? Either way, just being able to create (and manifest, which to me is the allowance of it into the here and now) a free parking space in a crowded lot will be a stretch for many of you. So, again, you might choose to start small. And, either way – large or small – just your continued focus will be putting in your cosmic order for "miracles" to happen. Yea, right?

♥ *Fear can close the door on your dreams. But, if you take down the door, fear has no place to go but away.*

♥ *What do you believe is possible? What do you believe is possible for YOU? Are they the same?*

♥ *Why would you try to create and manifest anything if you don't believe it is possible? When were you first told that it wasn't possible? Perhaps a church teaching… perhaps your community… perhaps your friends… perhaps, perhaps, perhaps. You have the right to choose for you. What's it going to be?*

Today I will think of someone in need and envision them surrounded by love.

This is a simple technique that can really make a difference for someone else. *Love is a universal life changer.* And within the energy of unconditional love is a power like nothing you have ever seen. It is the power of the Divine Energy of Creation.

I enjoy seeing love as represented by a beautiful pink mist, like cotton candy. You can envision it any way you like. There is no wrong choice. There are no rules. Just relax, close your eyes, and intend for your soul to show you what is the best choice for you now. Then, see the person (or animal) you chose surrounded and embraced by that vision.

Remember, though, that you do not have the right to make choices for others. Each of us has free will. It is our Divine right to choose how we will experience this human adventure. Have your intention be that you are sending unrestricted, unconditional love and that the person's choices are honored.

You may see the mist or light or energy you send not being allowed in, or being diverted, or you may get that sense. That's fine. You did your part. That is all there is for you to do. As you become more experienced, you will want to fully and consciously be aware of your connection to your soul and to the Divine Energy of Creation as you do this. Choice Point Creation Arts (accessing the Divine Energy of Creation via art) helps you to be able to instantly and effortlessly do this. From this space, sending love to someone can facilitate the

♥ *What does it feel like to know your potential to have a positive impact on others is unlimited? What choices will you make knowing that about yourself?*

miracle you desire for them. But, begin where you are. As you are ready, more will be made clear to you.

Use this technique at work, in a meeting, with your pets, with the grocery store clerk, when you hear a fire truck or an ambulance go by, for the earth, for water, for humanity... The options are unlimited. Your potential impact is unlimited.

♥ *You are more powerful and impactful than you could ever imagine. Would you like to direct that energy?*

Today I will say the Choice Point Creation Arts mantra out loud and with feeling.

I choose love.	I allow love.	I AM love.
I choose joy.	I allow joy.	I AM joy.
I choose peace.	I allow peace.	I AM peace.

I was offered this *mantra* by the Divine Energy of Creation to help shift me out of negative thinking immediately, and immediately raise my vibration and frequency. The net result being to add to my positive Universe order rather than dilute that order with less than positive thinking and feeling.

♥ *Feelings are the fuel for the fire of creation.*

Love and joy and peace are extraordinarily high in vibration. When we consciously and deliberately choose them and allow them into our thoughts and feelings, we tell our subconscious to shift our beliefs to support them in everyday life. Our subconscious begins to look for things in our everyday life that it can use to do just that. And, the Universe takes note of your desire and the "life order" you placed.

When you then acknowledge that you ARE love and joy and peace, you teach and reinforce yourself on every level of you that you are a part of the Divine Energy of Creation. As part, you ARE the Divine Energy of Creation (along with all other life). That is incredibly powerful. That shifts non-supportive beliefs into supportive beliefs automatically. You begin to actually feel the power of those statements - I AM love, I AM joy, I AM peace – and you begin to remember them as truth. As that happens, you begin to believe that you can actually create your reality – consciously and with intent. And you move into your full connection with the Divine Energy of Creation in the here and now. How awesome is that?!

♥ *I AM love. I AM joy. I AM peace. Yea!*

Today I will use the Choice Point Creation Arts mantra every time I experience discord and/or have a decision to make.

I choose love.	I allow love.	I AM love.
I choose joy.	I allow joy.	I AM joy.
I choose peace.	I allow peace.	I AM peace.

♥ *I choose love. I choose joy. I choose peace.*

♥ *I allow love. I allow joy. I allow peace.*

♥ *I AM love. I AM joy. IAM peace.*

Saying this mantra, even silently to yourself, will shift you out of negativity and into a higher vibration immediately. It works every time for me. Then, when you have a decision to make and or you experience discord, you are dealing with it from that energetic space of love and joy and peace and not from fear or anger or confusion.

Write this down on a card and keep it with you if it helps at first. You can get it laminated. Then, if needed, just whip it out and read it with feeling. Feeling is the fuel for thought. *When you infuse negative thought and energy with high vibrational energy and thoughts, the negative is no longer sustainable. Negative thoughts feed on fear. Don't feed them that!* Offer them love, joy, and peace. They will either rise to the occasion or leave. Either way, you win.

Today I will choose my own personal mantra.

I believe that this particular offering is so important that I do not want to limit what you choose for you to what I had chosen (by my soul) for me. To that end, I have compiled a list of choices that you might want to work with to choose your own personal mantra. What fun! Yours can be the Choice Point Creation Arts mantra or you can customize your own. Personally, I like what I have but I will add in others on particular days, in particular circumstances, or depending on the tone I want for my day.

1. I choose love.
2. I choose joy.
3. I choose peace.
4. I choose beauty.
5. I choose good abundance (Note: Abundance can be "good" or "bad" – you could have an abundance of cockroaches in your home for example!).
6. I choose the most expanded truth and understanding.
7. I choose clear and direct connection to my soul.
8. I choose clear and direct connection to the Divine Energy of Creation.
9. I choose a harmonious relationship with my body and all consciousness within. (Your cells have consciousness as do bacteria, your organs, etc.)
10. I choose music.
11. I choose color.
12. I choose touch and texture.
13. I choose water.
14. I choose air.

♥ *Your personal mantra can shift your vibration instantly. It is a quick and amazingly effective game changer.*

15.   I choose earth.

16.   I choose fire.

17.   I choose nature.

18.   I choose kindness.

19.   I choose compassion.

20.   I choose inner and outer sight.

21.   I choose to hear the beauty of life.

22.   I choose to taste the beauty of life.

23.   I choose to smell the beauty of life.

24.   I choose to feel the beauty of life.

25.   I choose to be awesome.

♥ What's your pleasure today?

26.   I choose wonder and awe.

27.   I choose playfulness.

28.   I choose creativity.

29.   I choose life.

30.   I choose to create my life consciously.

31.   I choose me within the Divine Energy of Creation.

32.   I choose the Divine Energy of Creation.

33.   I choose freedom.

34.   I choose harmony.

35.   I choose balance.

36.   I choose connection with all life.

37.   I choose tenderness.

38.   I choose to allow.

39.   I choose to embrace.

40.   I choose to embody.

41.   I choose to expand love.

42.   I choose to see life through the eyes of the Divine Energy of Creation.

43.   I choose to feel life as the Divine Energy of Creation.

44. I choose to love myself.
45. I choose to BE.

That should provide you with a good jumping off start to love, joy, peace and spiritual connection! Enjoy!

♥ *You are the designer of you. You are the art of you. You are beautiful inside and out. Own that!*

Today I am Superwoman (Wonderman)!

You already are amazing. You already are Superwoman/ Wonderman. Now. Yes, you! But, you have forgotten. You have been conditioned and taught otherwise over time, and your experiences have often backed up that thinking. Why? Because over time you began to lose faith in yourself. You developed beliefs that indicate you aren't worthy and you aren't powerful. Does that make it true though? Only if you continue to believe it!

♥ It's so easy to feel you have no power, no voice, no authority, no purpose. But, I would offer that you do have all those things. The first step is to believe it may be possible and then imagine that it is. Allow the feelings of self-empowerment, self-love, self-worth, self-AWESOMENESS to flow through your veins, nourishing you, revitalizing you, re-creating the you as the you that you want to be. For so it is if you allow it to be...

You are a part of the Divine Energy of Creation – the maker of all. You are both part of and you ARE that energy. How could that be if you are not worthy and amazing and powerful? The thing is, your focus is on a pinpoint of time – now – where you may be experiencing what feels like a lack of power.

Today, if this feels like you, switch gears. Imagine yourself to be amazing and awe-inspiring with incredible superpowers. Imagine what it would feel like for that to be true. Allow that feeling to be your truth today. Expect to be able to handle anything that comes your way with effortless ease. Expect to have a great day. Expect to be the creator of your day, exactly as you desire it.

If you already know your soul truth, expand on it and bring all that understanding and love and power into the now. Have it fill your day. Have it guide your day. Have it color your day beautiful and amazing and extraordinary and allow gratitude for that to be expressed in a variety of ways. Open to the experience. And allow it to flow. Wonderful, isn't it?

Today I will acknowledge those who have gone before me.

Some of us have a tendency to want to learn about things and to create from scratch instead of building on the learning and understandings and creations of others. When I began my spiritual journey, I questioned most things. I didn't blindly take anything as pure truth. It was a "show me the money" kind of thing. I wanted to see for myself. I waited a long time before I began to read what others had written about the things I was interested in knowing about. I wanted to find my own truth first so I'd have a foundation I could believe in, even if I chose to change my thinking later.

However, many people want others to share everything they know and then they want to tweak it or expand on it to suit them. That certainly is a more efficient way to do it! But, how often do those wonderful minds with original thought get the accolades they deserve. For a select few, they are abundant. For many others, they shared and were either forgotten or discarded.

I would offer that we tend to do the same with ancestors. All that we have and know was built upon the experiences and understandings and creations of those who came before us, in some capacity or another. Sometimes it's just the desire to have a better mousetrap. Other times it provides a substantial base from which to add new technology or new capabilities.

So, today, just take a moment to thank all those who have gone

♥ You are a part of all life everywhere. That's an AMAZING thing to contemplate. If we are all part of the Divine, we are all part of each other too. When you appreciate another, you also acknowledge value within yourself. Another win-win!

before you for their contributions. Take it back to the beginning of time. This will alert you about *our intricately linked consciousness, our linked lives, our linked experiences, our linked commonalities.* That's very important as you come to know yourself as a part of the Divine Energy of Creation – the energy of all life combined – and AS the Divine Energy of Creation.

♥ *When I say we are all part of the Divine and, thus, all connected, does that make you squirm? Are you thinking about those who do unspeakable things and how you DO NOT want to be a part of them or even remotely connected? If so, know that at the core of the Divine Energy of Creation, there is ONLY love. That's the point of connection. So, relax. You're good.*

Today I will gift the earth.

The earth is your friend. The earth is your supporter. The earth is your partner. The earth can be your mentor. Give the earth a gift today.

What do I mean by that? Well, in general, there are lots of ways we regularly gift the earth, but we may not give it those words. We may use and/or support solar power. Perhaps you recycle. Are you using only what you need? It is important to be respectful of the earth and all she offers. With that comes the conscious acknowledgement of respecting her. How can you give back today?

♥ *Our earth is a fabulous gift! She is amazing beyond compare. Let's share the love and honor her as she so richly deserves!*

Plant a tree. Pick up trash. Set up a compost bin. Explore how you can control bugs (insects are part of nature and the earth) in your home without hurting them (Example: Ants hate the smell of cinnamon. Mix cinnamon bark oil - not cassia - with water and spray where they are coming in. I laugh seeing them, in my mind, holding their noses and running. This is much better than other alternatives, it works, and your home will smell delicious!). Research complementary plants that control insects in the garden. Marigolds help with bugs on tomatoes, and they are beautiful. So, does that spark some ideas for you today? There are so many options!

This expansion will help you remember to appreciate the earth and all her many gifts every day. That, in turn, will open you to joy and an expanded level of love for your home for now - the earth.

Today I will gift my most favorite person (choose one if you have many!).

People love to be loved. People love to know that they are loved. People love to feel loved. Wouldn't it be easy to let someone know they are loved today? Send a text. Pick up the phone. Schedule coffee or a playdate. *Step into the power that comes from knowing that you can make someone feel special today.* You can make someone's day just by being you and connecting. Allow this expansion to remind you of how easy it is to share love and impact someone else's day in a lovely way. Love is. Shared love is x2 (at least).

♥ *How awesome is it that you can just be you and have the potential to completely change someone else's day in a lovely way? That rocks!*

Today I will gift my least favorite person.

YESSSSS really. And, not begrudgingly. Would you offer that they were doing the best they could with where they were physically, mentally, emotionally, and spiritually at the time? Would you offer that you don't know the person's entire story? Would you offer that you've grown in your understanding of love, and that you're willing to offer your current understanding of forgiveness based on that? What can you offer? Even if it is in your heart only, what can you offer? Are you willing to send them love? Are you willing to "forgive" them? Would you be willing to acknowledge that both sides played a less than optimal role? What can you offer? P.S. This is for you, not them.

♥ *When you release the energies of hurt, disappointment, anger, despair, and the like, you are saying "I love myself more." I hope you do!*

Life can be whatever you want it to be!

True Sight Expansion

True Sight Expansion is designed to unlock the doors to your heart. It is designed to allow you to safely be you. It is designed to help you to begin to fully allow the love of others to touch you deeply. For as you do that, so do you touch the authentic and most expanded version of you – the you that is part of the Divine Energy of Creation and thus, a part of all life.

♥ *Awareness is key to being and feeling in the now moment. The now moment is where you consciously create. What do you have planned for you to create today?*

Today I will reach for the stars and stretch to the earth.

Our connection to our bodies and to the earth is so important. *It is important to be in the now moment to consciously create.* To do that, it helps to be centered within the body. That means that you envision your heart as the center of the body with everything else receiving from the heart. This is actually and literally happening within as the heart communicates with the brain and as the sympathetic and parasympathetic systems within the body come into sync and balance. When you can consciously become aware of that and help facilitate that, it will resonate within your body as awareness, alertness, peacefulness, joy, and being present in your life. From that space, you become aware of your ability to create your experiences purposefully

and deliberately. *You step out of the role of reacting to life and into the role of creating your life.*

Exercise helps with syncing the body's systems and aligning them with the natural rhythm of the heart, especially as related to the emotions. The beautiful stretching movements, done with awareness and contemplation, of reaching for the stars and then stretching to the earth help with centering you in the heart. You become aware of your relationship with the earth. And you become aware of your body in relationship to it. *Awareness is key to being and feeling in the now moment.* So, take a moment to purposefully reach and stretch, appreciating the gifts around you and feel how your body and your emotions shift in response.

♥ *Would you rather react to life or create your life?*

Today I will embrace my day open to love in all forms, giving and receiving.

I have found that many are quite restrictive in how they will allow love. I believe this comes from not truly understanding the nature of love. Through our experiences and learning and what we've been taught, we can come to some skewed understandings of what love is and isn't. For example, if you grew up in a household where your parents withheld affection as punishment, you may think that is a normal expression of love in a relationship. It doesn't fit my definition of love.

Love is. The most expanded version of love is unconditional, limitless, all-inclusive, powerful yet gentle... As you will notice, I am not giving you a firm definition. I am offering descriptions. There is a continuum of love. Where you are tapping in on that continuum will offer you different versions of how love expresses. (Think of it like an upside-down pyramid or an ice cream cone. The tiny point is where most people make their choices and have their current understandings. The top and beyond offers a lot more variety and choices, and is more encompassing of those choices and understandings.)

Where I believe you desire to be is embracing and knowing and Being ALL of that continuum and beyond. It is tapping into the Divine Energy of Creation beyond time and space. It is connecting to your most expanded truth – that you are a part of that energy – the Divine Energy of Creation (the energy of all life as One) – and you ARE that energy. Be open to the possibility that this is true. Being part of the Divine

♥ *Are you ready to view life through the filter of love instead of the filter of fear? Are you willing to allow yourself to know your soul as your partner and view your ego as a tool you can partner with instead of a force over which you have no say? Your choice. Choose wisely.*

♥ Are you ready to really step into partnership with your soul and embrace all the benefits and wonder and awe of that? Let art and imagination help show you the way. Relax into love. Relax into knowing. Relax into you. You already have everything you need. Will you accept it? I'm here supporting you as you choose. Let the fun begin! Paint the portrait of you. Weave the tapestry of you. Dance the dance of you. Sing the song of you. You are the conductor of the symphony of you, you are the orchestra, you are the audience, and you are the music. What's your pleasure?

provides you with access to all the combined knowledge, all the combined power, all the combined knowing. Yet, here and now, our worthiness and beliefs and the beliefs we have been taught about our relationship with the Divine hold us back from that access.

If you would like to change those beliefs, begin with the Divine Energy of Creation – God, Source, Allah, etc. (I call these your "God beliefs") Are those beliefs serving you? Are they helping you feel connected to that energy? Begin to look at all creation (plants, animals, humans, the stars and planets, everything) as creations of that energy and as an expression of love. Begin to open to the concept that everything is love. Begin to open to sharing in its many myriads of expression. Love pours to you regularly every day. Begin to recognize that connection and be willing to accept it. A smile. A hug. A kind gesture. A phone call. A puppy's kiss. An unexpected surprise. The sun on your face. The wind in your hair. I think you are getting the point. *Everything is love and the giving and receiving of love is everything.*

Yet some of you will go "But what about the 'bad' things?". I would offer that in an expanded version of understanding there are no bad things. They are just things, just experiences, just opportunities to choose. Even those that appear to be horrific are included, at the most expanded understanding, since everything is love at its core. However, individuated expressions based on fear as the filter, can show differently from what we expect as love. That doesn't mean the action is accepted. It means, though, that you can see the action as coming from that person's filter of fear. That shifts your underlying feelings and emotions. It doesn't mean approval or acceptance. Only that you are seeing truth more clearly and from a more open view of love. That allows you to choose your response from a place further along the continuum – more towards the top of that continuum will offer you a better outcome than a choice made from fear.

You came here to experience. You came here to create. You had a life plan before you took the leap to show up here. What are you creating? What are you attracting into your life through your thoughts, feelings, and beliefs? These exercises are designed to shift your default thinking into those embracing love and joy and peace and kindness and compassion and good abundance and fun. They are designed to automatically reroute the neural net in your brain for "new" defaults. As you have new defaults, you view your experiences differently and you make different choices. Those choices are made from a space *of viewing life through the filter of love instead of the filter of fear.* Love begets love. Love responds to love. By choosing and allowing and giving love, you are actually creating more to come. So today, become aware of giving and receiving love in a variety of ways with no limitations or restrictions. Go!

♥ Life will dance a beautiful tango with you if you will participate.

Bottom Line

1. Everything is love.
2. All interactions are expressions of giving and receiving love.
3. Love has no limitations or restrictions.
4. Love is on a continuum.

5. The most expanded understanding of love is understanding yourself to be a part of the Divine Energy of Creation (the energy of all life combined) and that you ARE that energy, as is all life everywhere.

6. Expressions of love appear differently depending on where you are in your understanding of love.

7. You are love.

♥ *What if all you needed was love and all was love? Another win-win!*

Today I will be engaged with life.

What could I possibly mean? Well, how often do you just do things without thinking? For example, did you think about brushing your teeth when you brushed them this morning? When you made the kids sandwiches, did you just do it automatically as you were rushing to get out of the door, or did you actually think about what you were doing?

We tend to put many safe and benign tasks on automatic. It gives us brain space, or so we think.

♥ What do you love? What brings you joy? What makes you happy to be alive? Are your choices supporting those things? If not, are your choices made from love and not fear?

But what if noticing and being engaged with everything you do during the day enhanced the experience? What if living in the moment and being fully present was opening your eyes to the many joyful "miracles" around you? What if being engaged with life made you feel more alive and vibrant and connected? I offer that it will if you will allow it.

As you become engaged with life, you see the work of the Divine Energy of Creation in everything. Your body is incredible. How often do you think of all that goes on "behind the scenes" as you do activities? Have you ever watched a fern unfurl or a flower open? Have you ever stopped long enough to smell the earth as the rain comes down? Have you ever really looked at a dragonfly's wings or the markings on a honeybee? We live in such a diverse and amazing world with such beautiful things happening and presenting all around us moment by moment. Do you notice them? For today, make a conscious effort to do so.

For me, I'm going to go inhale the deliciously fragrant aroma of a cup of coffee. Will you join me?

Today I will see myself, who I really am, from the perspective of the Divine Energy of Creation.

How do you think the Divine Energy of Creation (God, Allah, the Universe, Source, etc.) sees you? You may have subconscious beliefs that tell you otherwise, but I will offer that you are loved beyond measure. I will offer that there is nothing to be forgiven. I will offer that you create/co-create with this energy. (You create via your desire and your feelings, but you simultaneously co-create since in 3D you need the energy of the whole - the Divine Energy of Creation - and hence, all of life, to have the energy and understanding and wherewithal to gather all the component parts together in a way to literally create what you desire and to bring it into your reality now.)

♥ When you consciously define yourself as love, joy, and peace, you are acknowledging your Divine heritage.

At the "choice point" of creation, before you came into physical form, you chose what you wanted to experience and some parameters around how you wanted it to play out. In the remembering of that choice, you open to the Choice Point Creation Arts energy. It is the energy at that choice point when you, as a part of and as the Divine Energy of Creation, chose your desire and made it happen. You open to being able to consciously access that energetic space to change things that you no longer desire. There is such empowerment in that. You are not a victim. You never have been, even if it felt like it.

Today, see yourself as loved, and loving, and powerful, and capable, and joyful, and peaceful, and whole. See yourself from that perspective today. If you don't yet believe it, imagine it. That imagination will open the creative flow to your more expanded awareness where everything is possible. That is the focus of Choice Point Creation Arts. It is using the creative energy of imagination to connect to your own Divinity and all that holds. Art, in its multitude of varieties, is a safe and accepted way to tap into imagination and the energy of creativity. It allows you to relax into being held and supported and encouraged by the Divine, knowing you are already enough, you are already loved beyond measure. You have nothing to prove. There is nothing to do but allow yourself to use art to bring you joy and gratitude and allow your soul connection to become conscious and deliberate – a choice – a choice to own your authentic self and to empower your human consciousness with Divine wisdom and understanding and truth and love. That's what it's all about. Are you ready to make that step in consciousness? Are you ready to really BE you? I think you are.

♥ *Are you ready to BE you?*

Today I will look at my life and see if there is a time when I have allowed someone else to influence me to act or live in a way that is not true to how I feel. I will decide if I want that to continue, with clear conscious choice. Or, I will decide to change it in a kind and loving way.

♥ *When you choose out of fear, that choice is not honoring you.*

♥ *Are you "the boss of you"? No? Well now… it might be a good time to re-evaluate and give yourself a promotion and raise! I KNOW you deserve it! Kindness begins with you. Be kind to you. Love you. Choose you. You're #1!!! Yea!*

We all make choices based on what we think is best in any given moment. *Many of us consider others and their feelings and needs and desires when making these choices.* And, for those reasons, we decide if we will stay true to what we believe and know, or not.

Now, I will say that sometimes, a choice where your voice is not as brilliant and melodic as usual is the kind and compassionate thing to do. But, when you consciously choose that as a gift for another, the energy of that isn't undermining you. It is supporting the virtues of kindness and compassion within you. However, it is important to re-visit such choices regularly to ensure that you have not become resentful or angry about it/them and that you now feel there is no way out.

So, back to allowing someone else to influence you… sometimes we allow others to negatively influence us (and by that, I mean staying authentic to the core of you and what you believe and enjoy) out of fear. It could be the fear of rejection, the fear of not being loved, the fear of being judged, the fear of not fitting in, the fear of not living up to the expectations and desires of others, and so on. When you choose out of fear, that choice is not honoring you. And everything about that choice holds the energy of that fear – even if it doesn't outwardly appear as fear to you.

Imagine what that does to your energy, especially over time. Yikes! No wonder you are tired. No wonder you are grumpy. No wonder life just seems to throw you curveballs all the time. No wonder…

So, look at you. What do you love? What brings you joy? What makes you happy to be alive? What choices have you made related to others that do not support those things? Are you ready to change?

♥ You have the power and right to change your situation anytime. If you choose to change it, will you claim the strength and courage to make that change…virtues you already possess?

Today I will write a love letter to myself.

Who better than you to write a love letter to yourself? You know you better than anyone else. But... oh no! I can hear some of you now. I'm not worthy. What have I done that makes me special? What do I have to offer? Look at how I've lived my life. I'm not loveable! NO! Just stop right now.

♥ What do you love about you? I can tell you something I love about you... Just by reading this, you have chosen you. That's awesome and I love that about you!

♥ Have you ever looked in the mirror and said, "I love you"?

You are an amazing Divine Being having a human experience, complete with all the mud and sweat and tears. What you have done and what you have experienced is not who you are. It's what you have experienced. It's what you chose at the time with where you were physically, mentally, emotionally, and spiritually. That's all. That doesn't make it all positive. But, it doesn't make you bad or unworthy or unlovable or less Divine. It just is part of your experience. And, there are ways to balance less than positive energy and choices with positive energy and choices. And, that begins with you loving you. The Divine Energy of Creation is only love. Your soul is part of that and IS that. You are a projection of your soul to a focal point of expression. Are you able to love you from there?

Today, think of you and write to you what you love about you. Let's begin, or continue, a positive uplifting loving and joyful understanding of you. Because it is you. It's not what you've done. It's not what you've chosen. I'm talking about you at your core, at your essence. Because when you can love yourself from that view, you can love others from that view, even if you don't agree with them and even if you can't fathom their choices. It's where you begin. With you.

Today I will write a love letter to the Divine Energy of Creation (God, Creator, Allah, the Universe, Source, etc.).

Many times, our feelings about ourselves are based on how we feel about the Divine. *We judge ourselves based on how we feel we measure up to Divine standards.* And, we can be brutal in that assessment.

What if the Divine loved you unconditionally – no matter your choices, no matter your actions, no matter your accomplishments or lack of accomplishments? What if that love was always and forever, and never lessened? How would you feel about you and the Divine then?

♥ *Love is a universal life changer.*

We are taught through our ancestors, our culture, our religions, our social groups, our family, our friends, and even strangers what we "should" believe and what we "should" do and how we "should" live. And that may or may not be aligned with the most expanded truth. What if it isn't? Or, what if only parts of it are in full alignment and represent truth?

If you believe that the Divine Energy of Creation is pure unadulterated, unfiltered, unrestricted, unconditional love, then what do you believe originates from that source? Only things based on love, right? You originated from that source. So, you are from pure love. As you as a soul desired experience and you projected a touch of your essence into the here and now, the more dense energy made it more challenging for you to remember what is real and distinguish it from what seems real.

As you begin to live in joy and love and peace more and more, you begin to tap into what your soul knows more and more. *Your soul loves the Divine -and also and thus - loves itself and all others and all life everywhere.*

Today, think about what you truly feel about the Divine and express that in a letter. It will help you clarify your own beliefs. *When you create your life, the energy is from that space where nothing but love exists and nothing but that that is from love can birth.* To truly understand this will help you create here and now. You and the Divine Energy of Creation are One and individual. Walk hand in hand with the Divine. It is who you are.

♥ *What would it feel like to consciously walk hand-in-hand with the Divine every moment of your day? If you believed that to be true, what would you desire? What would you want to accomplish? Now ask yourself why you aren't on that path right now...What's holding you back? What's the fear?*

Today I will gift the Divine Energy of Creation.

If you have walked with me along this wonderful pathway to the Divine so far, you should have a pretty good idea of what this would mean for you and how to do it. What do you have to offer the Divine? What will you gift you?

Be creative and do something wonderful, kind, compassionate, loving, joyful and amazing! Any time you do that, you are gifting both yourself and the Divine. Pretty awesome, right? And easy. Isn't it great to know that you have the power to bestow gifts to everyone in such a beautiful way? Can you imagine the difference you can make as you shift into consciously doing that as a way of life? I can. You rock!

♥ *How do you see your relationship with the Divine?*

♥ *The gift of you is the most amazing gift you have to offer. And, let there be no doubt. You are AMAZING!*

Today I will allow Divine wisdom and clarity to guide me.

In other words, today, actively and consciously listen to your intuition. "I don't have any!" you say. Well, I beg to differ. I offer that you do have the full component of intuition already. But, for whatever reason and on whatever level, you are not allowing it to reach your conscious awareness. That's fine, though. Doing these simple fun exercises, over time, will shift your beliefs and thoughts enough that your intuition will make itself known.

♥ Have you had a Godwink today?

♥ What if the first step wasn't the hardest? What if the first step was exciting? Your choice.

Have you ever felt like your stomach was in knots when you heard something? That's your intuition telling you to be careful. Have you ever had a fleeting thought before you decided to make a choice, but you just disregarded it? That's your intuition showing you the best way. Do you ever have feelings of unease when you meet someone? Again, that's your intuition. Do you ever think of someone and then they call? Have you ever listened to something and then it shows up in your life? Do you ever read something, and you are drawn to it, and then that information is relevant to you soon after? You are probably more allowing of your own intuition than you know. Start to notice. And, when you notice, pay attention and follow the queues.

Lastly, be grateful when you notice your intuition at play. Gratitude is a high vibrational feeling. Begin to live in a state of gratitude and watch how more of what you are grateful for shows up. Just remember to really feel it and not just say it to yourself – though that is a beginning. Begin where you are and go from there. As the saying goes… if you don't take that first step…

Today I will embrace my day with less resistance than yesterday, and I allow more of my soul energy to guide my day than yesterday.

Many people feel that they are always pushing against life. Things come into their experience and it always feels like a struggle. If this is you, it is your life that you are resisting. Perhaps it is moving forward with a plan. Perhaps it is taking ownership of your choices. Perhaps it is being willing to let others know how you really feel. Perhaps it is about not wanting to be seen – the real you, and not what you present to others as the real you. It could be a variety of things, and it could be more than one at a time.

What I have found is that if you choose (and decide to act on that choice) to allow your soul energy to guide you, you will begin to notice things that you never would have noticed before. A level of synchronicity will appear. It may show up in something you read or hear or watch. It might show up in what someone says or who calls and when. Doors and pathways begin to open for you so that what you want becomes easier to have. If you are just beginning to explore your relationship with your soul energy, I have a helpful tip. Go to the bookstore and find an inspirational book. It helps if it is a book of quotations (some of my favorites are listed in Favorites at the end of this book). Then, when you would like to know the direction in which your soul wants you to go, set an intention that you will open the book to a page that will offer that insight and you will be drawn to the location on the page that is most appropriate. It worked beautifully for me and seemed to be perfect every time.

♥ Why would you choose struggle when you can have grace and ease? You have a spiritual team available to assist you and your soul is ever ready to have you be conscious of your partnership. We have come to believe that through the struggle, we learn more and have a better understanding of the issue. But, what if that was not true? What if you could learn and experience joyfully with an equal or greater level of clarity and understanding? Would you be all in? If so, climb aboard. The soul train is leaving the station!

Your soul will not guide you into a state of resistance. *Resistance is your response, based on your beliefs and feelings, to fear of some type.* You are hard wired to work to stay safe in this world. Fear comes with an understanding that you are not safe. So, you resist what you believe will cause you fear and that feeling of not being safe. That is the resistance. So… the next time you feel that you are having to push against life and that life is a struggle, pause. Breathe. Take a moment and ask yourself what the fear is about. Go with the first thing that comes to you even if it seems unlikely or far-fetched. Then ask yourself when that fear first originated. Then, explore that situation with new vision, with an expanded view of what fear is really about. Why are you allowing that past fear to rule you? What is causing you to not feel safe? Really dig deep to get to the core truth of the matter. Recognition is the first step to resolving the hold it has on you. Every day, life is pointing you in the direction that you need to look. Pay attention. Ask your soul for assistance and then be on the lookout for tips and help. *The expectation of assistance alone will help to open the connection to your soul's most expanded expression.*

♥ *Every day, life is pointing you in the direction that you need to look. Pay attention.*

Today I will live authentically to the best of my ability, honoring what I believe and feel to be true.

You may have a tendency, as many do, to allow thoughts and expectations and judgements and perceived judgments to choose what you do and how you present yourself to others. You came to believe that it served you to have the approval of others to the exclusion (or dampening) of your own desires and choices. So, you allowed it to the point that you might not even know what you want and think and know anymore.

Today is a chance to recognize any level of that within you (it may be only in one area of your life and/or you may not even have recognized that about yourself) and to act on it. You make the choices today, as best you can, to complement and support what you want and what you need and what you believe. Today is only about you and not others. What do you choose for you?

♥ If you know you better than anyone else, you would be the best person to choose for you, right? If you aren't, why aren't you? What do you love? What makes your heart sing? What makes your body smile? What makes your ego relax? Those answers will be the breadcrumbs back to authenticity if you have lost your way.

♥ You are the designer of you. Recognize when the design needs a tweak and then tweak it. You will discover what you value about you and what you do not. It's all changeable. You only need pertinent information. That comes from observing and paying attention. It's so worth the effort!

Today I will expect to see the real me as reflected back to me by others and what happens in my life. I will accept what I see without judgment or self-pity.

Who ARE you? Do you have a good sense of who and what you are? Most people think of themselves as the persona they have developed. They don't even know how to know who they really are. So, how do you uncover that? One simple technique is to look at how people relate to you and see their actions and reactions as reflections of you.

♥ Have you ever thought about who you are and why you are here? We want our boxes to be tidy and stacked just so. But what if the purpose was to get back to the freedom to be anything you wanted to be? What if life was about the experience and learning and embracing what is in the moment? Just a bit of food for thought…

Others react, consciously or not, to the energy you are presenting. The energy doesn't lie, distort, or mask. It just is. So, if others are showing up in your life with anger, explore where you are angry and are allowing that energy to present. If others show up presenting kindness and compassion, explore how you feel those same energies and explore how you can facilitate more of that in your life.

Don't be upset by anything you uncover. This is just fact finding and exploration. It's you helping you to feel better and be better.

Today I will be present.

What does it mean to be present in your life? So many times, we are not living in the moment. We are thinking of what has already happened and/or we are thinking of what we expect is going to happen. But, the present – the now – is where you are creating your future through your thoughts and feelings. *Stop living in the past and future and live in the now. Create – consciously – in the now.*

For some of you, this particular exercise will seem very challenging at first. You may feel like if you don't think of the past and the future, you are sticking your head in the sand and you will be left reacting to life.

But pause for a moment... are you doing that right now – reacting to life? My goal is to help you understand and begin to consciously create what you desire by living in joyful expectation, joyful gratitude, play, and being aware of what you are thinking and feeling. When you are aware, you can change the thoughts and feelings you do not choose for your creation. Those little pesky rogue thoughts will cease, with practice.

Remember the "No. I choose love." expansion where you used that phrase whenever you had a thought not based in love? Keep doing that for a little while and you will find that you rarely have to anymore. You told the Universe you wanted a different kind of thought and the accompanying feelings and that's what begins to show up for you. It's the same thing on any scale.

♥ *The world and your experiences in the world can be awesome and magical and wonderful and expansive and creative – if you allow it to be. Is there anything holding you back from that truth? If so, time to do some dusting!*

So today, be present. Know what you are thinking and feeling and change your thoughts and feelings to fit what you would like your day to be like. That's right! Do it on the fly as you go through your day! You've got this! I have faith in you. Do you have faith in you?

♥ *Living and being aware in each moment brings forth the beauty and richness and depth of life. From there, you can choose what you fancy and what you would like to consciously create by aligning your thoughts and feelings and actions to your desires. Happy fun creating!*

Today I am blessed with the power of the Universe and I feel that power as I make my choices.

You may not feel powerful. You may not feel that you have control over life and what it brings. But, what if you were powerful and what if you did have control in that you knew you created all that comes into your life? How would that make you feel? Imagine it now. But, imagine it without using that feeling to hold fear at bay. What if you knew that you didn't need power to push fear away? What if you knew that how you act and what you think and feel today is what was sent out into the Universe by you as your order for tomorrow and the future? What if you knew that by thinking thoughts originating out of love and joy and peace and kindness and feeling the associated emotions, that you were ordering that for your future? Wouldn't that be great?

Well, for today, imagine that to be true. As you go through your day, feel powerful. Make choices that resonate with love and joy and peace and kindness and feel those things as you make those choices. Because, you will find as you do this more and more, your life will begin to reflect it back to you more and more. Automatically. Teach yourself to live in a state of love and joy and peace and kindness. It may feel uncomfortable at first. It may feel weird - but do it anyway. You may not feel genuine when you do it at first. Do it anyway with the understanding that it is a first step towards personal power and Universal understanding of how energy works. Be happy that you are on your way to your own unique personal greatness and creative life. Allow this to work as a first step for you. Be brave.

♥ Allow the energy of your soul to color your day beautiful and amazing and extraordinary. Be the most incredible artist of you! Let your soul shine!

♥ Power has been misused by some forever. Our beliefs around power can be complicated, as the abuse of power by others factors in. What if, however, there was a power based only in love and from which only love could birth? Would you embrace it then? YOU already are that power. Your soul offers you more than you can possibly imagine. Are you ready to create and co-create your life consciously? Imagine what it would feel like to be a force for love and joy and kindness and compassion.

Today I will see the blessings of my life path and allow my heart to fill with gratitude.

We don't always look at how our life is playing out with excitement and joy. In fact, sometimes, it can be very discouraging. But, remind yourself that you chose the experiences you wanted to have. Your free will allows you to choose how you will perceive them and how you will let them impact you. And, it allows you to change aspects of your experience that you no longer desire.

♥ A miracle is merely you being in perfect alignment (and being harmonized and balanced) with your soul. In that space and energy, EVERYTHING would seem like a miracle – even though none of it would actually be miraculous. It would just be what is.

The first step is to fill your heart with gratitude. See everything that happens to you today as a message from the Divine Energy of Creation and be thankful. Know that as you feel gratitude, you are raising your vibration and that will shift what comes your way. Step into the "feeling" of gratitude as much as you possibly can. It's not just the words or thoughts, it's the feeling. Feelings are powerful. Your entire body responds to them. Your mind can distinguish between a feeling it has come to know as good and one it has come to know as bad. It responds by sending the appropriate neurochemicals throughout your body. That impacts you on so many levels.

Find something good to say about everything that happens to you today, even if it seems silly. For example, if your coffee spills on your clothes, be thankful it didn't scald someone else or that all of it didn't spill or that the cup didn't break. You get the drift. Find a good thing about it even if it doesn't seem like anything you would ever admit to a friend. This is for you only for right now. However, you'll find that with practice, you will soon eagerly be helping others to spot things to be grateful for. You may even have to curtail your enthusiasm a bit because people will wonder about you! Enjoy today. If you allow, this technique can literally change your life.

♥ *You are blessed by the Divine beyond measure. Allow yourself to know that.*

Today I allow the purity of my soul to bring me peace.

You are a Divine Being having a human experience. I believe we are focal point expressions of our souls. And, I know we can invite in the wisdom and unconditional love and supreme peacefulness and exquisite joy of our soul into the here and now.

♥ Peace is such a joyous feeling. It goes from the tiniest speck of you to the greatest expanse of you. It is total trust in the Divine and in yourself. It is such a gift. Accept this gift and unwrap it with reverence and appreciation.

You have been learning and experimenting with touching your soul. You have been reaching out to your soul. Your soul hears you every time. Your soul knows you and loves you intimately with no reservations, no limitations, no boundaries, and no anything else. You and your soul are One right here and right now. The key is to become aware of the Light and love and wisdom of your soul and work and play hand-in-hand here and now. That connection and awareness is incredibly peaceful. You know you are safe in every way. You know there is no real death. You can relax. You can let go. Do it today. Allow it to fill you. Feel your heart open to the truth. Feel it expand from your heart throughout your body. You are Divine. You are already enlightened. You are perfect. You are amazing. Allow all that in. Disregard what you believe about you from your earthly experiences and know yourself from your soul perspective. It will give you a fresh new way to view the world and you in it. And, it is peaceful and joyful and filled with unrestricted love.

You deserve this. Will you accept it?

Today I will be aware of my Spidey * sense.

We have been building up to a time when you are willing to allow in your intuitive gifts – your Spidey sense. Today, be aware when things just match up, coincidences happen, life just flows and is so easy, things just drop in your lap (things you want!), and the world seems brighter and more beautiful. Today, be aware about how you feel when you interact with individuals. Pay attention to the feeling. It's more important than the words, and often more important than the actions. Just be in a state of excited expectation of wonderful flow in your life and see what happens. Be grateful and feel grateful whenever you notice something like this. These are your Spidey senses having fun.

♥ *Who knew Spidey senses had fun? Woohoo!*

* Nod to Marvel comics.

Today I will fly.

Today just let go. Just allow life without attempting to control it. Just enjoy it all and notice how it plays out. Expect wonderful. Radiate wonderful. Enjoy wonderful. You can do this!

♥*What if you had wings... What kind would they be? What color would they be? Would you feel empowered? Would you feel special? That said, imagine flying WITHOUT wings! You can... if you believe you can. Imagine it. Feel it. Believe it. There are many types of flying just so you know...*

Today I will meet a spiritual guide and receive a message.

We each have a lovely spiritual contingent available to assist us for the asking. Don't let this spook you! There are many types of assistance if you so desire.

A lovely way to get messages from a guide is to do a short guided meditation. Are you ready? Okey dokey. Get comfortable and close your eyes. Take a few deep breaths and release each with sound. Then, imagine yourself on a beautiful beach (or in a lovely mountain field if you'd rather). As you walk down the beach, take everything in. What does it smell like? Do you feel the salt spray on your face? Is it warm? Is it sunny? Do you see shells at the waterline? Take it all in. As you walk, you look up and see a person walking towards you. What does the person look like? Is the person male or female? What is the person wearing? The person has a message for you. When the person gets to you, ask them what the message is and thank them for bringing it to you. When you are ready, open your eyes. You just met one of your guides! What message did he or she bring? How do you feel about it?

♥ Wonderful is the word of the day! Wonderful you. I wonder how wonderful the day will be!

♥ I love angels. Do you? Four-legged angels are especially amazing! Just so you know…

You can also envision a treasure chest waiting for you on the beach. Open it and find what awaits you.

Yet another easy way to receive a message is to get out a spiritual book (perhaps one with quotations or short messages) and intend to get the right message for you when you open the book. Allow your eyes to be guided to the place on the page where your message awaits. Read your message and give thanks for the assistance.

The way you receive messages may well vary and may change over time. When you truly come to believe that you can receive valid messages and assistance from your spiritual team, you will find that you no longer need to use a meditation or a technique to access them. They just "drop in". Using a technique and getting validation at first will help you to release your fears and disbelief.

Be sure to intend to only accept messages that are aligned with your most expanded and best truth. I word it that way because you may not be able to accept – yet – the Divine's most expanded version of truth. Go with where you are in the moment and it will shift, and you will automatically become more aligned with the most expanded truth on the continuum of truth.

Working with your spiritual contingent or team is so much fun and very helpful – especially as you have decisions to make. Be open and be thankful. Both will go a long way.

♥ *Your spiritual team has a sense of humor too – if that's how you roll. If you enjoy humor, you will likely find that as you begin to receive effortlessly, you find incredible humor within the presentation at times. In no way does this lessen the spiritual and Divine nature of the assistance. It just shows how much you are loved and how comfortable your spiritual team wants you to feel. Relax into it. Fun is still reverent and relevant – if you allow it to be. Your choice. Be brave. Be bold. Enjoy! You've got this!*

Today I will envision what it looks and feels like to be a part of all life and be me - a unique individual.

Part of reconnecting to wonder and awe is to open the pathway to your soul. *From the soul perspective, you are enlightened, amazing, incredible, wonderful, and joyful beyond measure. You have all the clarity and wisdom and power you need. And, it is peaceful. You are also connected to all life everywhere.* To be able to allow that understanding into the 3D experience, it helps to be able to envision what that would be like.

Imagine what it would look and feel like to be an individual and be directly connected to all life everywhere. How does that make you feel? Does it feel expansive or restrictive? Does it feel comfortable or not? What does your heart say?

♥ From the spiritual perspective, being part of the whole doesn't diminish your uniqueness and individualism.

If you need a bit of assistance here, close your eyes and imagine a beautiful white ball of Light within your heart. Watch as this Light expands and fills your entire body. Feel it as it fills every cell and all the space in-between. See this Light expand from your heart and from your body to fill the room you are in. Imagine the entire world engulfed in this beautiful Light and you are merged with it all. Then see this Light continue to the stars and then the Universe and then continuing on forever, all the while connecting you with all life.

This expansiveness will help you become familiar with the truth of your soul. From that space, it is hoped that you will allow it to return with you to the here and now, filled with clarity and truth and wisdom, so you can create your best life.

Today I will design my own meditation.

At the beginning of this book I told you that you were your own guru. You are. You know you better than anyone else. To assist you to believe that about you, today is a day for designing your own meditation.

Where do you think all the various meditations come from? They come from people just like you who were inspired in a moment and took pen to paper and wrote down a lovely way to access the Divine and/or a more peaceful state. For the purposes of today, the definition of a meditation is a visualization where you imagine how you will feel better or act with more kindness or assist with world peace or whatever suits you. Write it down and then do it. Write it as if you were writing it for someone else.

Here's an example.

Close your eyes. Get relaxed. Take a deep breath in and breathe out all your cares and worries. Take a deep breath in and breathe out all negative emotions and feelings. Take another deep breath in and release with sound. Imagine that you see a magic carpet waiting for you. Imagine that the magic carpet knows right where to go to show you what you need to know today. Step onto the magic carpet and get comfortable. Feel the carpet lift off, knowing you are completely safe and will easily find your way back. Look down and see where you are going. What do you see? Is it familiar? How does it make you feel to see it? Watch as your special magic carpet is landing. Now that it has landed, step off. Where are you? What time in history is it? Do you recognize anything? Do

♥ Designing your own meditation is very freeing and empowering. You have everything you need to create a beautiful meditation to fit your needs. Happy creating!

you recognize anyone? Allow what you need to know to be revealed to you with grace and ease, knowing you continue to be safe. When you are through and have what you needed, step back on the magic carpet and allow it to safely return you home. Know that you can take a magic carpet ride anytime you want, and you will always be guided to the best time and location for you and you will always be loved and safe. When you are ready, open your eyes.

It's all about using your imagination to create a safe space for you to accomplish what you desire to accomplish with a meditation of this type. It's easy to design your own. Like the beach? Design yours around that theme. Prefer a mountain meadow? The choice is yours. Happy imagining!

♥ When the heart and the mind work together in unison and with harmony and balance, when the ego is a supportive partner, anything is possible. You set the vision. You have the desire. You align with the energy of the realization of that desire. You create and manifest. You are grateful to all as the One. Woohoo! You rock! Conscious creation is birthed from love. It is birthed from you at your expanded soul level. You can change the world. Are you ready to own that? I would love that for you.

Today I will congratulate myself on choosing to find and celebrate myself and life!

Hooray! Happy dance! Congratulations! You chose to choose you. You chose to do the best for you to reconnect with wonder and awe as a pathway to re-connection to your truth that you are already enlightened! Thank you for allowing me to participate! I am happy for you and I encourage you to continue your journey. Opening to your spiritual gifts is amazing and fun. Let art and creativity in their many forms open the pathway wider and to keep it open for you. As long as you are here, there will always be more. Enjoy the journey. You deserve it! Happy happy joy joy and then some more!

♥

Thank you for being you and choosing me to walk
this journey with you. I am honored. Many blessings
of wonder and awe and joy and connection...

Let the awesomeness of you touch the awesomeness of me and let's play!

♥

Your choice.
Your design.
Your creation.
Your art.
Your life.
What's your pleasure today?

♥

What Now?... or It's Not Over!

Part of my goal with this book is to help anyone who wants to be able to connect more fully with his or her soul to do so, here and now. I fully believe that this can be done, with some re-training and re-wiring, without years of study and practice. Your connection to your soul will bring forth your intuitive gifts, love, joy, peace, infinite wonderful abundance, and the understanding and clarity to know that you can consciously create your life and what you experience.

I believe we can use the energy of creativity and our emotional connection to various types of art and creative endeavors to teach ourselves how to consciously achieve that high state of awareness and receptivity, without the need to become immersed in art and creative endeavors every time. Yet, those endeavors and that immersion feel safe and doable and provide us with a fun and enjoyable and "allowed" way to begin to access all of the intuitive gifts that we already possess and have available to us. It's training your brain and your ego that it is safe and OK to do so. It happens automatically when you become so immersed and in love with what you are involved with artistically and creatively that you lose track of time and your only focus is the flow of creative energy and how good that makes you feel. When you've done that enough to KNOW that safety and you know what it feels like, you can consciously choose that connection any time and any place and apply it in any way you choose.

The practices I have shared with you here are a way to become centered within your body and within your heart. They are designed to align, balance, and harmonize all your systems and energy bodies so that you can focus on designing and creating your life consciously.

One way to use this book as you progress after this journey is to intend to open it to a page that will show you what you need for the day. Then open the book and follow its lead.

I am so glad that you chose to walk with me through this reconnection to wonder and awe and your intuitive gifts. You are ALREADY enlightened. Open your heart to love and joy and peace to connect to your soul and the Divine Energy of Creation and you will come to understand the truth of that and be able to honor that as you live here and now.

Mahalo (may you be held in the breath of God) and I hope we meet again,

Linda

♥

And so it is if you create and allow it to be…

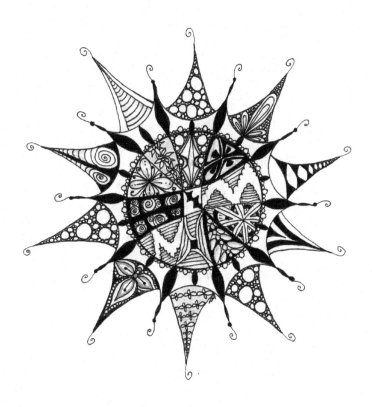

It doesn't get better than you being you! You are AMAZINGLY wonderful!

♥

Your choice.
Your design.
Your creation.
Your art.
Your life.
What's your pleasure today?

♥

Some of My Favorites

https://www.choicepointcreationarts.net No surprise here I'd bet! Occasionally, Choice Point Creation Arts will offer workshops and other offerings. Hope to connect again!

For more scientific information:

The Intention Experiment by Lynne McTaggart

Want to know more about the science of all this and what studies have been going on for a long time? Read this book. I have underlined so much and dog-eared the pages so many times that I might as well not have done any! Lynne McTaggart is an award-winning journalist. She assembled her thoughts based on multiple interviews or correspondence with medical doctors and/or scientists and others. Everything is documented thoroughly, and her conclusions lead us right to the core of the issue in a very logical way. I love this book! It's not a story. It's not a book that deals with the subjective or feelings. It's about science and medical knowledge and using that to test the power of intention. I have recommended it to all my students. And, I am recommending it to you if you are curious about how what I have shared actually works, outside of the personal, subjective and anecdotal evidence.

There are many more books that now offer a scientific perspective on the spiritual. Yea! But, the one above shows how long the research has been going on and it was the first one I came across.

For books/quotations to use to get a message from Spirit:

<u>Reconnecting to Wonder and Awe - A Spiritual Playbook for Bringing the Wisdom and Energy of Your Soul into the Everyday to Create Your Best Life</u> I like this one the best! I bet you aren't surprised one bit!

<u>Gifts from A Course in Miracles</u> edited by Vaughan and Walsh

If you've ever tried to read A Course in Miracles, you may have found it to be overwhelming at first. I love this book because it is formatted in very concise points from the original book. It's very easy to read and I highly recommend it for just opening to a page to receive guidance.

The <u>Bartholomew</u> series is great. They are channeled offerings.

The <u>Emmanuel</u> channelings are great.

The <u>Spiritual Unfoldment</u> series is also another favorite by White Eagle.

<u>Abraham</u> is a current version of channeled offerings. You can go to that website and sign up for daily messages to be emailed to you. You may be amazed at how very relevant they are.

I recommend reading all of these! And, keep them for reference. Wonderful. And, I have another one of these in the works too! Be on the lookout!

For additional techniques to address beliefs

ThetaHealing® is a powerful avenue for expanding your knowledge about beliefs, feelings, healing, and connection. It provided a turning point for me on my personal journey.

https://www.thetahealing.com

Emotions

Emotions are powerful. Yet, we don't always acknowledge them. We are amazingly talented at hiding things from ourselves that would cause us fear or pain or other unpleasant feelings. A spiritual counselor friend suggested that working with a body map that identifies where emotions are typically held in the body has been used with a lot of success.

The National Academy of Sciences of the U.S. offers research in this area of study. https://www.pnas.org/content/111/2/646 They offer you body graphics that show where you are most likely to hold various emotions. If you are having issues and aren't having success identifying the cause, locating the area of the body impacted and then referencing that with the body maps of emotions might help you see that you are holding onto an emotion and didn't even recognize it. If you can then associate the emotion with an event or situation, you will be better able to release and resolve it. This might be a good interim step until you have spent time with the exercises in this book such that negative emotions automatically resolve and/ or are not able to sustain within your vibration.

This is similar to using the scale of emotions. With the scale, when you are feeling an emotion, you find an emotion higher on the scale than the one you are experiencing and consciously change your feelings to the higher vibration. In other words, if you feel fear, if anger is the next emotion on the scale, try your best to feel angry instead of fearful. Go as high up as you can go to shift your emotion into a higher vibration.

Love and gratitude and happy dancing!

♥

Your choice.
Your design.
Your creation.
Your art.
Your life.
What's your pleasure today?

♥

Acknowledgements

First and always would be the Divine Energy of Creation (God, Allah, Source, the Universe, etc.) and those in Spirit who love and surround and assist me (and you!). I am here and I am able to share with you because of them - and you, because you are a part of the Divine (the energy of all life combined) and because you were drawn to share this journey with me.

I am thankful for the ThetaHealing® technique and the other various studies and classes and offerings I have had over the years. I am thankful for all my teachers - even the unintended ones! I am thankful for all the people who have allowed me to assist them over the years because I always learned from each interaction. And, I am thankful for the art of Zentangle® that helped me to break free of the self-imposed limitations I had about art.

I am thankful to Nature and all her gifts and thankful for all those on the human, animal, and plant journeys.

Many thanks to those beautiful friends who were and are so encouraging and helpful - Dawn Lindsey your enthusiasm and insight and energy were amazingly helpful; Lisa Danso-Coffey your love and centeredness and care flow through everything you do and I value it all; Terri Hollingsworth your encouragement and wisdom and wonderful perspective are so very appreciated and were very helpful; Luz Fry your insights and love are unstoppable and treasures, but I especially appreciate you showing me the value of relatability via stories, a long time ago; and Cathy Boytos, beautiful Light and tangle guru; my Balboa team; and others who helped in various ways to get this offering published. And I am thankful to my husband and pups who support me and love me non-stop.

All these together got me to here - now - and to the birthing of Choice Point Creation Arts and this book. And, finally, I am thankful to me! I worked diligently on myself and I am thankful for all the progress I have made and am continuing to make on this life journey.

Thank you all! You rock!

About Me

Interestingly enough, this is a multi-tiered consideration! I am a person just like you. I am on a journey of spiritual and life exploration and understanding. It is a dynamic, always changing, journey. And, I have decided to live it in joy and love and peace.

When I began the spiritual part of my journey, I was connected to about as much intuitive ability as a rock - and the rock may have had more! So many of the students in the many various classes I took were having these amazing experiences connecting to the Divine Energy of Creation (God, Source, the Universe, Allah, etc.) but me, not so much. But, some pull within me kept encouraging me to keep trying. I sometimes felt abandoned by the Divine. I sometimes felt like it just wasn't worth it. But, that pull was still there so I kept with it.

I think my biggest breakthrough was when I began my ThetaHealing® journey. I found a tool that I could use to work on myself. I had no intention of doing anything with it other than that. But, I decided to take the teacher training, mainly so I could meet the founder. After that training, I felt compelled to share the technique and began to teach.

Over time, I learned many things about myself and about how there were many people who had amazingly similar issues. Most of those issues were a direct result of being disconnected from the energy of the Divine. They could say the words. They had the desire. But something was in the way.

As I changed that for myself, I began to see how I could help others change in a very direct easy and fun way. I kept being reminded by Spirit that I was here in this world and to be aware of that and enjoy that in the now. I kept being shown the beautiful everyday miracles, like a flower opening or the sound of a bird or the yummy taste of chocolate. And, I began to understand that all that was equally as important as the "woo woo" stuff (which we all love!). And then art come into my life.

A friend asked me if I wanted to go to a "doodle" class with her. Well, no of course not! And, naturally, I smiled kindly as I declined! But, when my husband came home after seeing my friend at an event and mentioned that he thought I'd love this class, I paid attention. I have learned that there really are no coincidences. I know! "Heresy!" some would say. But, I know there is a Divine plan at work behind the scenes for each of us. Those seeming coincidences are just your Spirit team encouraging you in one direction versus another. So, I changed my mind and said yes to a Zentangle® class.

Though I had been good (in my humble opinion!) with crafts, drawing and other types of "art" were way outside my comfort zone. But my friend was right. Zentangle® is fun! I play with it all the time now and it has opened my horizons to painting and freestyle drawing. Who knew "doodling" could offer so much! In any case, all that worked together to show me that, if you live in the moment, if you use art to connect to your innate creative nature, and if you do things that bring you happiness and joy, your life can automatically shift into living from the heart in a state of love and peacefulness, and that good abundance just shows up in every way. And, then I was moved to share that with others and, hence, Choice Point Creation Arts was birthed.

I have training in a number of energy healing techniques (beginning about 35 years ago! Oh my!) and have taught and worked with people for a number of years. But, this fun and extraordinarily powerful way to reconnect to wonder and awe - Choice Point Creation Arts - is where my heart is now. I open that to you with joy and gratitude.

♥

Your choice.
Your design.
Your creation.
Your art.
Your life.
What's your pleasure today?

♥

Printed in the United States
By Bookmasters